Ninja Creami Deluxe High Protein Recipes Cookbook

1500 Days of Plant-Based Fruits, Low-Calorie, Sugar-Conscious, Low-Carb Recipes' for Healthy Living

By

Sophia E. Hayes

© 2024 Sophia E. Hayes

Table of Contents

PROTEIN CHOCOLATE CHIP COOKIES
PROTEIN ALMOND JOY BITES
PROTEIN OATMEAL RAISIN COOKIES
PROTEIN MINT CHOCOLATE TRUFFLES
PROTEIN SNICKERDOODLE ENERGY BALLS
PROTEIN COCONUT MACAROONS
PROTEIN CHOCOLATE BARK
PROTEIN CHOCOLATE-COCONUT TRUFFLES
PROTEIN-PACKED RICE KRISPIE TREATS

CHAPTER 9: CREAMY CREAMICCINOS RECIPES

VANILLA PROTEIN CREAMICCINO
CHOCOLATE PROTEIN CREAMICCINO
CARAMEL PROTEIN CREAMICCINO
MOCHA PROTEIN CREAMICCINO
HAZELNUT PROTEIN CREAMICCINO
RASPBERRY VANILLA PROTEIN CREAMICCINO
BLUEBERRY PROTEIN CREAMICCINO
PEANUT BUTTER PROTEIN CREAMICCINO
BANANA PROTEIN CREAMICCINO
COCONUT PROTEIN CREAMICCINO

CHAPTER 10: ITALIAN ICE CREAM

LEMON BASIL ITALIAN ICE
STRAWBERRY BALSAMIC ITALIAN ICE
MANGO COCONUT ITALIAN ICE
RASPBERRY LIME ITALIAN ICE
WATERMELON MINT ITALIAN ICE
PINEAPPLE COCONUT ITALIAN ICE
BLUEBERRY LEMON ITALIAN ICE
PEACH MANGO ITALIAN ICE
KIWI LIME ITALIAN ICE
MIXED BERRY ITALIAN ICE

CONCLUSION

Introduction

Welcome to the Ninja Creami Deluxe High Protein Recipes Cookbook, your complete guide to making delicious and nutritious frozen desserts in your own home! This cookbook is filled with delicious recipes that highlight the versatility and possibilities of the Ninja Creami Deluxe, a powerful blender that allows you to easily whip up creamy, high-protein treats.

In today's fast-paced world, keeping a healthy lifestyle without sacrificing flavor can be difficult. That's where the Ninja Creami Deluxe comes in, providing a simple way to make handmade sweets that are not only delicious but also high in protein and healthy nutrients. Whether you're a fitness buff looking for post-workout snacks or a dessert fan looking for guilt-free options, this cookbook has something for everyone.

Inside these pages, you'll find a variety of recipes, from velvety Creamiccinos to cool Italian Ice Adventures, all precisely made to satisfy your taste buds while nourishing your health. We've provided thorough instructions, nutritional information, and serving advice for each recipe, so you can easily make tasty frozen treats that meet your dietary needs and objectives.

So take your Ninja Creami Deluxe and prepare to go on a gastronomic trip full of protein-packed delicacies that will leave you satiated and wanting more. Whether you're throwing a summer party, rewarding yourself after a long day, or seeking for a healthy alternative to store-bought desserts, this cookbook includes everything you need to unleash your creativity and reap the sweet rewards.

Chapter 1

Understanding the High Protein Diet

In recent years, high protein diets have become popular among health-conscious people, athletes, and fitness fanatics. But what precisely is a high-protein diet, and why is it good? Let's start with the basics to understand the importance of protein in our diets.

1. Proteins have a crucial role in life. They are necessary for the development, healing, and maintenance of tissues in our body. Proteins are composed of amino acids, some of which are considered essential since our bodies are unable to manufacture them and must be received through diet.

2. Benefits of a High Protein Diet:

• Protein helps grow and repair muscular tissues, making it vital for physical exercise and strength training.

• High protein diets improve satiety, leading to longer-lasting feelings of fullness and satisfaction. This can help with weight management by lowering overall calorie intake.

• Adequate protein intake leads to enhanced metabolic health, including better blood sugar regulation and lower risk of metabolic diseases.

• Protein promotes bone health by maintaining density and strength, especially as we age.

3. Protein intake recommendations vary depending on age, gender, activity level, and health goals. However, a general recommendation is to ingest 0.8 to 1 gram of protein per kilogram of body weight. Higher protein intake may be recommended for people who engage in intense physical exercise or muscle growth.

4. Protein can come from both animal and plant sources. Animal protein sources include lean meats, poultry, fish, eggs, and dairy products. Plant-based options include legumes, tofu, tempeh, nuts, seeds, and whole grains. Including a variety of protein-rich foods in your diet ensures that you get a full range of amino acids.

5. Balancing macronutrients: While protein is vital, it is also necessary to consume a well-balanced diet rich in carbohydrates, fats, vitamins, and minerals. Balancing macronutrients maintains dietary adequacy and promotes optimal health.

Understanding the importance of protein in our diets, as well as the benefits of high protein intake, allows you to make more informed meal selection and preparation decisions. The recipes in this cookbook are intended to help you fulfill your protein needs in a delicious and healthy way, whether you're looking to build muscle, lose weight, or improve your general health.

Tips for Using the Ninja Creami Deluxe

The Ninja Creami Deluxe is a multipurpose kitchen equipment that allows you to easily create creamy, tasty, and protein-packed dishes. Whether you're blending smoothies, making ice cream, or whipping up protein drinks, these suggestions will help you make the most of your Ninja Creami Deluxe.

1. For recipes requiring a chilled or frozen base, such ice cream or smoothies, pre-chill the ingredients before mixing. This results in a smoother texture and guarantees that your frozen delicacies are ready to consume right away.

2. Use High-Quality Protein Powders: To add protein to your recipes, choose high-quality powders with a neutral or complementing flavor. This guarantees that your protein-packed dishes taste delicious and offer the nutrition you require.

3. Experiment with Flavors: Be creative with flavor combinations! To create distinctive and delectable taste profiles, combine fruits, nuts, spices, and extracts in your recipes. Mix and mix items to find your favorite combinations.

4. When creating layered desserts or parfaits, arrange components strategically for esthetic appeal. For a visually appealing presentation, begin with a protein-rich base, then layer in fruits or nuts and conclude with a creamy topping.

The Ninja Creami Deluxe allows you to customize the consistency of your recipes. For thicker textures, use less liquid or incorporate frozen components. For smoother blends, use more liquid and blend for a longer period of time.

6. Regularly clean and maintain your Ninja Creami Deluxe for best performance and longevity. Follow the manufacturer's maintenance instructions. Proper cleaning avoids residue buildup and keeps your equipment in good condition.

7. Freeze leftover smoothies, ice cream, or shakes in individual amounts for quick and easy snacks or desserts. Simply thaw when ready to consume, or combine them again for a refreshing treat.

8. Experiment with Recipe Variations: Many dishes can be tailored to your dietary needs or constraints. To build personalized recipes that match your specific

requirements, substitute components, tweak quantities, or experiment with other preparation methods.

By implementing these recommendations into your Ninja Creami Deluxe use, you'll be able to maximize its performance and make a variety of high protein meals that are both delicious and nutritious.

Equipment & Tools

To get the most of your Ninja Creami Deluxe and create delicious high-protein meals, you should have the proper equipment and utensils on hand. Here are some important factors to consider:

1. Ninja Creami Deluxe. This multifunctional equipment is the foundation of your culinary creativity. The Ninja Creami Deluxe's blending, whipping, and freezing features make it simple to produce smoothies, ice creams, shakes, and other frozen treats.

2. High-Quality Blender Blades: The Ninja Creami Deluxe features powerful blades for crushing ice, blending fruits, and creating creamy textures. Ensure that the blades are sharp and in good condition for the best blending results.

3. Use accurate measuring cups and spoons to achieve the desired consistency and flavor in your recipes. Keep a set of measuring cups and spoons on hand to ensure correct ingredient quantities.

4. Choose high-quality protein powders based on your dietary and flavor preferences. Options include whey protein, plant-based protein (such as pea or soy protein), collagen peptides, and others.

5. Stock up on frozen fruits and vegetables, including berries, bananas, and mangos, as well as spinach and kale. These ingredients are ideal for smoothies and provide natural sweetness and nutrition to your recipes.

6. Nut Butters and Seeds: Almond butter, peanut butter, chia seeds, and flaxseeds include beneficial lipids, protein, and fiber. They may make smoothies, shakes, and desserts more creamy and nutritious.

7. Silicone Ice Cream Molds: Use silicone molds to freeze individual quantities of homemade protein ice cream or popsicles. They're simple to remove and clean, so you can enjoy your frozen delicacies without effort.

8. Purchase blender bottles or shakers with mixing balls for convenient protein shakes or smoothies on the move. These containers make it simple to blend and transport your beverages wherever you go.

9. Food Processor Attachments: Some Ninja Creami Deluxe models include attachments for chopping nuts, mixing heavier mixes, and producing nut butters.

10. Storage Containers: Keep airtight containers on available for leftover smoothies, ready components, and homemade protein snacks. Glass and BPA-free plastic containers are good for food storage.

With these basic kitchen equipment and utensils, you'll be able to produce a variety of high-protein meals with your Ninja Creami Deluxe.

Advantages of Using the Ninja Creami Deluxe

1. The Ninja Creami Deluxe is a versatile device that can combine, whip, and freeze substances. This versatility enables you to make a wide range of high-protein meals, such as smoothies, ice cream, shakes, desserts, and more.

2. Customization: The Ninja Creami Deluxe gives you complete control over the components used in your creations. You can tailor the protein amount, flavor combinations, sweetness levels, and texture to your specific dietary choices and nutritional goals.

3. Healthy Ingredients: With the Ninja Creami Deluxe, you can create high-protein meals at home with fresh and healthful ingredients. Fruits, vegetables, nuts, seeds, protein powders, and other nutritious foods can be used without the addition of preservatives or artificial tastes.

4. Nutrient Retention: The Ninja Creami Deluxe's blending and freezing capabilities preserve the nutrients in your ingredients. This implies that you may obtain the entire nutritional value of fruits, veggies, and protein sources in your high-protein recipes.

5. Cost-effective: Creating your own high-protein foods at home can save money compared to purchasing pre-made protein items. You may buy ingredients in bulk, control portion proportions, and avoid paying for extra sugars or fillers that are commonly included in commercial products.

6. The Ninja Creami Deluxe encourages creativity in the kitchen. You can experiment with different flavor combinations, textures, and presentation methods to create one-of-a-kind and delightful high-protein dishes that cater to your tastes.

7. Time-saving: Despite its versatility, the Ninja Creami Deluxe prioritizes efficiency. It can swiftly combine, freeze, and serve your recipes, so you can enjoy delicious high-protein meals and snacks without having to spend hours in the kitchen.

8. Ninja Creami Deluxe allows for healthier alternatives to store-bought sweets and snacks. You have control over the ingredients, sugar content, and additives, making it easier to meet your health and fitness goals.

9. Family-Friendly: The Ninja Creami Deluxe is suitable for a variety of dietary demands and preferences. You can work with your family members to create and enjoy healthful high-protein foods together.

10. Sustainable practices: Making homemade high-protein meals with the Ninja Creami Deluxe encourages sustainable practices. You can reduce packaging waste, eliminate single-use plastics, and promote ecologically friendly food options.

Overall, utilizing the Ninja Creami Deluxe to prepare high-protein meals has various advantages that contribute to a healthier, more enjoyable cooking experience.

Chapter 2: Ice Cream Recipes

Protein-Packed Chocolate Peanut Butter Ice Cream

- **Prep Time:** 10 minutes

- **Cook Time:** 0 minutes

- **Serving Size:** 4 servings

Ingredients:

- 2 ripe bananas, sliced and frozen

- 1/2 cup plain Greek yogurt

- 2 tablespoons cocoa powder

- 2 tablespoons natural peanut butter

- 1 scoop chocolate protein powder

- 1 teaspoon vanilla extract

- Optional toppings: chopped peanuts, dark chocolate shavings

Instructions:

1. In the Ninja Creami Deluxe blender pitcher, combine frozen bananas, Greek yogurt, cocoa powder, peanut butter, protein powder, and vanilla extract.

2. Blend on the ice cream setting until smooth and creamy.

3. Serve immediately as soft-serve or transfer to a freezer-safe container and freeze for 1-2 hours for a firmer texture.

4. Sprinkle with chopped peanuts and dark chocolate shavings before serving, if desired.

Nutritional Information per Serving:

- Calories: 180 kcal

- Protein: 12g

- Carbohydrates: 24g

- Fat: 6g

- Fiber: 4g

Vanilla Almond Protein Ice Cream

- **Prep Time:** 5 minutes

- **Cook Time:** 0 minutes

- **Serving Size:** 4 servings

Ingredients:

- 2 cups unsweetened almond milk

- 1 scoop vanilla protein powder

- 1 teaspoon almond extract

- 1 tablespoon honey or maple syrup (optional for sweetness)

- Sliced almonds for garnish

Instructions:

1. In the Ninja Creami Deluxe blender pitcher, combine almond milk, vanilla protein powder, almond extract, and sweetener if using.

2. Blend until smooth and creamy.

3. Pour the mixture into the Creami Deluxe freezer attachment and freeze according to the manufacturer's instructions.

4. Serve topped with sliced almonds.

Nutritional Information per Serving:

- Calories: 90 kcal
- Protein: 10g
- Carbohydrates: 3g
- Fat: 4g

- Fiber: 1g

Berry Blast Protein Sorbet

- **Prep Time:** 5 minutes
- **Cook Time:** 0 minutes
- **Serving Size:** 4 servings

Ingredients:

- 2 cups mixed berries (strawberries, blueberries, raspberries)
- 1/2 cup plain Greek yogurt
- 1 scoop berry-flavored protein powder
- 1 tablespoon honey or agave syrup
- Fresh mint leaves for garnish

Instructions:

1. In the Ninja Creami Deluxe blender pitcher, combine mixed berries, Greek yogurt, protein powder, and honey.
2. Blend until smooth and creamy.
3. Transfer the mixture to the Creami Deluxe freezer attachment and freeze until firm.
4. Scoop into bowls and garnish with fresh mint leaves before serving.

Nutritional Information per Serving:

- Calories: 110 kcal
- Protein: 9g
- Carbohydrates: 15g
- Fat: 1g
- Fiber: 4g

Mint Chocolate Chip Protein Ice Cream

- **Prep Time:** 10 minutes

- **Cook Time:** 0 minutes

- **Serving Size:** 4 servings

Ingredients:

- 2 ripe bananas, sliced and frozen

- 1/2 cup plain Greek yogurt

- 1 scoop chocolate protein powder

- 1/2 teaspoon mint extract

- 1 tablespoon dark chocolate chips (sugar-free if preferred)

Instructions:

1. In the Ninja Creami Deluxe blender pitcher, combine frozen bananas, Greek yogurt, protein powder, and mint extract.

2. Blend until smooth and creamy.

3. Stir in dark chocolate chips.

4. Serve immediately for a soft-serve consistency or freeze for 1-2 hours for a firmer texture.

Nutritional Information per Serving:

- Calories: 140 kcal

- Protein: 10g

- Carbohydrates: 20g

- Fat: 3g

- Fiber: 3g

Peanut Butter Banana Protein Swirl Ice Cream

- **Prep Time:** 10 minutes
- **Cook Time:** 0 minutes
- **Serving Size:** 4 servings

Ingredients:

- 2 ripe bananas, sliced and frozen
- 1/2 cup plain Greek yogurt
- 1 scoop vanilla or chocolate protein powder
- 2 tablespoons natural peanut butter
- 1 tablespoon honey or maple syrup (optional)
- Dark chocolate drizzle (optional)

Instructions:

1. In the Ninja Creami Deluxe blender pitcher, blend frozen bananas, Greek yogurt, and protein powder until creamy.
2. In a separate bowl, mix peanut butter and honey or maple syrup until smooth.
3. Layer the banana ice cream and peanut butter mixture in a freezer-safe container, swirling gently with a spoon.
4. Freeze for at least 2 hours or until firm.
5. Drizzle with dark chocolate before serving, if desired.

Nutritional Information per Serving:

- Calories: 180 kcal
- Protein: 12g
- Carbohydrates: 22g
- Fat: 6g
- Fiber: 3g

Coconut Mango Protein Ice Cream

- **Prep Time:** 10 minutes
- **Cook Time:** 0 minutes
- **Serving Size:** 4 servings

Ingredients:

- 2 cups frozen mango chunks
- 1/2 cup coconut milk (canned, full-fat)
- 1 scoop vanilla or tropical fruit-flavored protein powder
- Shredded coconut for garnish

Instructions:

1. Blend frozen mango chunks, coconut milk, and protein powder in the Ninja Creami Deluxe blender pitcher until smooth.
2. Pour the mixture into the Creami Deluxe freezer attachment and freeze until firm.
3. Scoop into bowls and garnish with shredded coconut before serving.

Nutritional Information per Serving:

- Calories: 150 kcal
- Protein: 8g
- Carbohydrates: 20g
- Fat: 6g
- Fiber: 2g

Raspberry Cheesecake Protein Ice Cream

- **Prep Time:** 15 minutes

- **Cook Time:** 0 minutes

- **Serving Size:** 4 servings

Ingredients:

- 1 cup frozen raspberries

- 1/2 cup cottage cheese

- 1/2 cup plain Greek yogurt

- 1 scoop vanilla protein powder

- 1 tablespoon honey or agave syrup

- Crushed graham crackers for topping

Instructions:

1. In the Ninja Creami Deluxe blender pitcher, blend frozen raspberries, cottage cheese, Greek yogurt, protein powder, and honey until smooth.

2. Transfer the mixture to the Creami Deluxe freezer attachment and freeze until semi-firm.

3. Scoop into bowls and sprinkle crushed graham crackers on top before serving.

Nutritional Information per Serving:

- Calories: 120 kcal

- Protein: 11g

- Carbohydrates: 14g

- Fat: 3g

- Fiber: 4g

Banana Nut Protein Ice Cream

- **Prep Time:** 10 minutes

- **Cook Time:** 0 minutes

- **Serving Size:** 4 servings

Ingredients:

- 2 ripe bananas, sliced and frozen

- 1/2 cup unsweetened almond milk

- 1 scoop vanilla or banana-flavored protein powder

- 2 tablespoons chopped walnuts or pecans

- 1/2 teaspoon ground cinnamon

Instructions:

1. Blend frozen bananas, almond milk, protein powder, chopped nuts, and cinnamon in the Ninja Creami Deluxe blender pitcher until creamy.

2. Pour the mixture into the Creami Deluxe freezer attachment and freeze until firm.

3. Scoop into bowls and garnish with additional chopped nuts before serving.

Nutritional Information per Serving:

- Calories: 130 kcal

- Protein: 9g

- Carbohydrates: 17g

- Fat: 5g

- Fiber: 3g

Coffee Protein Frappe Ice Cream

- **Prep Time:** 10 minutes
- **Cook Time:** 0 minutes
- **Serving Size:** 4 servings

Ingredients:

- 1 cup cold brewed coffee
- 1/2 cup unsweetened almond milk
- 1 scoop vanilla or chocolate protein powder
- 1 tablespoon honey or maple syrup (optional for sweetness)
- Ice cubes (as needed)

Instructions:

1. Blend cold brewed coffee, almond milk, protein powder, and sweetener (if using) in the Ninja Creami Deluxe blender pitcher until smooth.

2. Add ice cubes and blend until the mixture reaches a thick and creamy consistency.

3. Pour the frappe into glasses and serve immediately.

Nutritional Information per Serving:

- Calories: 70 kcal
- Protein: 8g
- Carbohydrates: 3g
- Fat: 2g
- Fiber: 1g

Green Tea Protein Matcha Ice Cream

- **Prep Time:** 15 minutes

- **Cook Time:** 0 minutes

- **Serving Size:** 4 servings

Ingredients:

- 2 cups coconut milk (canned, full-fat)

- 1 tablespoon matcha green tea powder

- 1 scoop vanilla or unflavored protein powder

- 2 tablespoons honey or agave syrup

- Toasted sesame seeds for garnish

Instructions:

1. In a bowl, whisk together coconut milk, matcha powder, protein powder, and sweetener until smooth.

2. Pour the mixture into the Ninja Creami Deluxe freezer attachment and freeze until semi-firm.

3. Scoop into bowls and sprinkle toasted sesame seeds on top before serving.

Nutritional Information per Serving:

- Calories: 200 kcal

- Protein: 10g

- Carbohydrates: 10g

- Fat: 15g

- Fiber: 1g

Strawberry Banana Protein Nice Cream

- **Prep Time:** 10 minutes
- **Cook Time:** 0 minutes
- **Serving Size:** 4 servings

Ingredients:

- 2 ripe bananas, sliced and frozen
- 1 cup frozen strawberries
- 1/2 cup plain Greek yogurt
- 1 scoop vanilla or strawberry protein powder
- 1 tablespoon honey or agave syrup (optional)

Instructions:

1. In the Ninja Creami Deluxe blender pitcher, blend frozen bananas, frozen strawberries, Greek yogurt, protein powder, and honey until smooth.

2. Transfer the mixture to the Creami Deluxe freezer attachment and freeze until desired consistency is reached.

3. Serve immediately for a soft-serve texture or freeze for 1-2 hours for a firmer ice cream.

Nutritional Information per Serving:

- Calories: 130 kcal
- Protein: 8g
- Carbohydrates: 25g
- Fat: 1g
- Fiber: 4g

Blueberry Coconut Protein Ice Cream

- **Prep Time:** 10 minutes

- **Cook Time:** 0 minutes

- **Serving Size:** 4 servings

Ingredients:

- 1 can (14 oz) coconut milk (full-fat)

- 1 cup frozen blueberries

- 1 scoop vanilla or coconut-flavored protein powder

- 2 tablespoons shredded coconut

Instructions:

1. In a blender, combine coconut milk, frozen blueberries, protein powder, and shredded coconut until smooth.

2. Pour the mixture into the Ninja Creami Deluxe freezer attachment and freeze until solid.

3. Scoop into bowls and enjoy the creamy blueberry coconut flavor.

Nutritional Information per Serving:

- Calories: 180 kcal

- Protein: 8g

- Carbohydrates: 10g

- Fat: 15g

- Fiber: 2g

Caramel Pecan Protein Ice Cream

- **Prep Time:** 15 minutes
- **Cook Time:** 0 minutes
- **Serving Size:** 4 servings

Ingredients:

- 2 cups unsweetened almond milk
- 1 scoop vanilla or caramel-flavored protein powder
- 1/4 cup sugar-free caramel sauce
- 1/4 cup chopped pecans

Instructions:

1. Blend almond milk, protein powder, and caramel sauce until well combined.
2. Transfer the mixture to the Ninja Creami Deluxe freezer attachment and freeze until semi-firm.
3. Stir in chopped pecans and freeze until completely firm.
4. Scoop into bowls and drizzle with additional caramel sauce if desired.

Nutritional Information per Serving:

- Calories: 120 kcal
- Protein: 10g
- Carbohydrates: 5g
- Fat: 8g
- Fiber: 1g

Chocolate Mint Protein Ice Cream Bars

- **Prep Time:** 15 minutes

- **Cook Time:** 0 minutes

- **Serving Size:** Makes 6 bars

Ingredients:

- 1 cup plain Greek yogurt

- 1 scoop chocolate protein powder

- 1 tablespoon cocoa powder

- 1/2 teaspoon mint extract

- Dark chocolate chips for topping (optional)

Instructions:

1. In a bowl, mix Greek yogurt, protein powder, cocoa powder, and mint extract until smooth.

2. Pour the mixture into popsicle molds or an ice cube tray.

3. Insert popsicle sticks or toothpicks into each mold.

4. Freeze for at least 4 hours or until completely frozen.

5. Before serving, dip the frozen bars in melted dark chocolate and sprinkle with additional chocolate chips if desired.

Nutritional Information per Serving (1 bar):

- Calories: 60 kcal

- Protein: 7g

- Carbohydrates: 4g

- Fat: 2g

- Fiber: 1g

Banana Split Protein Ice Cream Bowl

- **Prep Time:** 15 minutes

- **Cook Time:** 0 minutes

- **Serving Size:** 2 servings

Ingredients:

- 2 ripe bananas, sliced and frozen

- 1/2 cup plain Greek yogurt

- 1 scoop vanilla or chocolate protein powder

- 1/4 cup diced pineapple

- 1/4 cup sliced strawberries

- 2 tablespoons chopped walnuts or almonds

- Whipped cream and cherry for topping (optional)

Instructions:

1. Blend frozen bananas, Greek yogurt, and protein powder in the Ninja Creami Deluxe blender pitcher until creamy.

2. Transfer the mixture to serving bowls.

3. Top with diced pineapple, sliced strawberries, chopped nuts, whipped cream, and a cherry.

4. Serve immediately as a delicious and nutritious banana split ice cream bowl.

Nutritional Information per Serving:

- Calories: 220 kcal

- Protein: 10g

- Carbohydrates: 30g

- Fat: 8g

- Fiber: 4g

Chapter 3: Gelato Recipes

Vanilla Bean Protein Gelato

- **Prep Time:** 10 minutes

- **Cook Time:** 0 minutes

- **Serving Size:** 4 servings

Ingredients:

- 2 cups whole milk (or almond milk for a dairy-free option)
- 1/2 cup granulated sugar or sweetener of choice
- 1 vanilla bean pod (or 1 tablespoon vanilla extract)
- 1 scoop vanilla protein powder

Instructions:

1. In a saucepan, heat the milk and sugar over medium heat, stirring until the sugar dissolves.

2. Split the vanilla bean pod lengthwise and scrape the seeds into the milk mixture. (If using vanilla extract, add it after heating.)

3. Remove from heat and let the mixture cool completely.

4. Once cooled, stir in the vanilla protein powder until fully incorporated.

5. Pour the mixture into the Ninja Creami Deluxe freezer attachment and churn according to the manufacturer's instructions.

6. Serve the gelato immediately for a soft texture or transfer to a freezer-safe container and freeze for a firmer consistency.

Nutritional Information per Serving:

- Calories: 180 kcal
- Protein: 10g
- Carbohydrates: 25g
- Fat: 5g

- Fiber: 0g

Chocolate Hazelnut Protein Gelato

- **Prep Time:** 15 minutes
- **Cook Time:** 0 minutes
- **Serving Size:** 4 servings

Ingredients:

- 2 cups heavy cream (or coconut cream for a dairy-free option)
- 1/2 cup granulated sugar or sweetener of choice
- 1/4 cup cocoa powder
- 1/4 cup chopped hazelnuts
- 1 scoop chocolate protein powder

Instructions:

1. In a saucepan, combine the heavy cream, sugar, and cocoa powder. Heat over medium heat, stirring until the sugar dissolves and the mixture is smooth.
2. Remove from heat and let it cool completely.
3. Stir in the chopped hazelnuts and chocolate protein powder until well combined.
4. Pour the mixture into the Ninja Creami Deluxe freezer attachment and churn according to the manufacturer's instructions.
5. Serve the gelato immediately for a soft texture or freeze for a firmer consistency.

Nutritional Information per Serving:

- Calories: 250 kcal
- Protein: 8g
- Carbohydrates: 20g
- Fat: 17g
- Fiber: 2g

Strawberry Cheesecake Protein Gelato

- **Prep Time:** 20 minutes
- **Cook Time:** 0 minutes
- **Serving Size:** 4 servings

Ingredients:

- 2 cups fresh or frozen strawberries
- 1 cup plain Greek yogurt
- 1/2 cup granulated sugar or sweetener of choice
- 1 scoop vanilla or cheesecake-flavored protein powder
- 1/4 cup crushed graham crackers

Instructions:

1. In the Ninja Creami Deluxe blender pitcher, blend the strawberries, Greek yogurt, sugar, and protein powder until smooth.
2. Pour the mixture into the Creami Deluxe freezer attachment and churn until creamy.
3. Stir in the crushed graham crackers for added texture.
4. Serve the gelato immediately for a soft texture or freeze for a firmer consistency.

Nutritional Information per Serving:

- Calories: 180 kcal
- Protein: 10g
- Carbohydrates: 25g
- Fat: 4g
- Fiber: 2g

Pistachio Protein Gelato

- **Prep Time:** 15 minutes

- **Cook Time:** 0 minutes

- **Serving Size:** 4 servings

Ingredients:

- 2 cups whole milk (or almond milk for a dairy-free option)

- 1/2 cup granulated sugar or sweetener of choice

- 1/2 cup shelled pistachios, finely chopped

- 1 scoop vanilla or pistachio-flavored protein powder

- Green food coloring (optional)

Instructions:

1. In a saucepan, heat the milk and sugar over medium heat until the sugar dissolves, stirring frequently.

2. Remove from heat and let it cool completely.

3. Stir in the chopped pistachios, protein powder, and green food coloring (if using) until well combined.

4. Pour the mixture into the Ninja Creami Deluxe freezer attachment and churn until creamy.

5. Serve the gelato immediately for a soft texture or freeze for a firmer consistency.

Nutritional Information per Serving:

- Calories: 200 kcal

- Protein: 9g

- Carbohydrates: 25g

- Fat: 7g

- Fiber: 1g

Cookies and Cream Protein Gelato

- **Prep Time:** 15 minutes

- **Cook Time:** 0 minutes

- **Serving Size:** 4 servings

Ingredients:

- 2 cups heavy cream (or coconut cream for a dairy-free option)

- 1/2 cup granulated sugar or sweetener of choice

- 1/2 cup crushed chocolate sandwich cookies (sugar-free if preferred)

- 1 scoop vanilla or cookies and cream-flavored protein powder

Instructions:

1. In a saucepan, combine the heavy cream and sugar over medium heat, stirring until the sugar dissolves and the mixture is smooth.

2. Remove from heat and let it cool completely.

3. Stir in the crushed chocolate sandwich cookies and protein powder until well combined.

4. Pour the mixture into the Ninja Creami Deluxe freezer attachment and churn until creamy.

5. Serve the gelato immediately for a soft texture or freeze for a firmer consistency.

Nutritional Information per Serving:

- Calories: 280 kcal

- Protein: 7g

- Carbohydrates: 30g

- Fat: 15g

- Fiber: 1g

Banana Nutella Protein Gelato

- **Prep Time:** 15 minutes
- **Cook Time:** 0 minutes
- **Serving Size:** 4 servings

Ingredients:

- 2 ripe bananas, sliced and frozen
- 1/2 cup milk (dairy or plant-based)
- 2 tablespoons Nutella or hazelnut spread
- 1 scoop chocolate or hazelnut-flavored protein powder
- Chopped hazelnuts for garnish

Instructions:

1. In the Ninja Creami Deluxe blender pitcher, blend frozen bananas, milk, Nutella, and protein powder until smooth and creamy.

2. Transfer the mixture to the Creami Deluxe freezer attachment and churn until it reaches a gelato-like consistency.

3. Serve immediately topped with chopped hazelnuts.

Nutritional Information per Serving:

- Calories: 200 kcal
- Protein: 10g
- Carbohydrates: 30g
- Fat: 6g
- Fiber: 3g

Raspberry White Chocolate Protein Gelato

- **Prep Time:** 20 minutes
- **Cook Time:** 0 minutes
- **Serving Size:** 4 servings

Ingredients:

- 2 cups frozen raspberries
- 1 cup heavy cream (or coconut cream)
- 1/2 cup granulated sugar or sweetener of choice
- 1/4 cup white chocolate chips (sugar-free if preferred)
- 1 scoop vanilla or white chocolate-flavored protein powder

Instructions:

1. In a blender, blend frozen raspberries, heavy cream, sugar, white chocolate chips, and protein powder until smooth.

2. Pour the mixture into the Ninja Creami Deluxe freezer attachment and churn until creamy.

3. Serve the gelato immediately for a soft texture or freeze for a firmer consistency.

Nutritional Information per Serving:

- Calories: 280 kcal
- Protein: 8g
- Carbohydrates: 25g
- Fat: 18g
- Fiber: 3g

Mango Coconut Protein Gelato

- **Prep Time:** 15 minutes
- **Cook Time:** 0 minutes
- **Serving Size:** 4 servings

Ingredients:

- 2 cups frozen mango chunks
- 1 can (14 oz) coconut milk (full-fat)
- 1/2 cup granulated sugar or sweetener of choice
- 1 scoop vanilla or coconut-flavored protein powder
- Shredded coconut for garnish

Instructions:

1. In the Ninja Creami Deluxe blender pitcher, blend frozen mango chunks, coconut milk, sugar, and protein powder until smooth.
2. Pour the mixture into the Creami Deluxe freezer attachment and churn until it thickens into gelato.
3. Serve immediately, garnished with shredded coconut.

Nutritional Information per Serving:

- Calories: 250 kcal
- Protein: 8g
- Carbohydrates: 30g
- Fat: 12g
- Fiber: 2g

Lemon Blueberry Protein Gelato

- **Prep Time:** 15 minutes

- **Cook Time:** 0 minutes

- **Serving Size:** 4 servings

Ingredients:

- 2 cups frozen blueberries

- Zest and juice of 1 lemon

- 1 cup plain Greek yogurt

- 1/2 cup granulated sugar or sweetener of choice

- 1 scoop vanilla or lemon-flavored protein powder

Instructions:

1. In a blender, blend frozen blueberries, lemon zest, lemon juice, Greek yogurt, sugar, and protein powder until smooth.

2. Transfer the mixture to the Ninja Creami Deluxe freezer attachment and churn until it reaches a gelato consistency.

3. Serve immediately or freeze for a firmer texture.

Nutritional Information per Serving:

- Calories: 180 kcal

- Protein: 9g

- Carbohydrates: 25g

- Fat: 4g

- Fiber: 3g

Matcha Green Tea Protein Gelato

- **Prep Time:** 20 minutes

- **Cook Time:** 0 minutes

- **Serving Size:** 4 servings

Ingredients:

- 2 cups whole milk (or almond milk)

- 1/4 cup honey or agave syrup

- 2 tablespoons matcha green tea powder

- 1 scoop vanilla or matcha-flavored protein powder

- Toasted sesame seeds for garnish

Instructions:

1. In a saucepan, heat the milk and honey over medium heat until the honey dissolves, stirring occasionally.

2. Remove from heat and let it cool slightly.

3. Whisk in the matcha green tea powder and protein powder until smooth.

4. Pour the mixture into the Ninja Creami Deluxe freezer attachment and churn until creamy.

5. Serve the gelato immediately topped with toasted sesame seeds.

Nutritional Information per Serving:

- Calories: 200 kcal

- Protein: 10g

- Carbohydrates: 30g

- Fat: 5g

- Fiber: 1g

Salted Caramel Protein Gelato

- **Prep Time:** 20 minutes

- **Cook Time:** 0 minutes

- **Serving Size:** 4 servings

Ingredients:

- 1 cup heavy cream (or coconut cream)

- 1/2 cup granulated sugar or sweetener of choice

- 1/4 cup sugar-free caramel sauce

- 1 scoop vanilla or caramel-flavored protein powder

- Pinch of sea salt

Instructions:

1. In a saucepan, combine the heavy cream and sugar over medium heat, stirring until the sugar dissolves and the mixture is smooth.

2. Remove from heat and let it cool slightly.

3. Stir in the sugar-free caramel sauce, protein powder, and a pinch of sea salt until well combined.

4. Pour the mixture into the Ninja Creami Deluxe freezer attachment and churn until creamy.

5. Serve the gelato immediately for a soft texture or freeze for a firmer consistency.

Nutritional Information per Serving:

- Calories: 280 kcal

- Protein: 8g

- Carbohydrates: 25g

- Fat: 18g

- Fiber: 0g

Almond Joy Protein Gelato

- **Prep Time:** 15 minutes
- **Cook Time:** 0 minutes
- **Serving Size:** 4 servings

Ingredients:

- 2 cups coconut milk (canned, full-fat)
- 1/2 cup granulated sugar or sweetener of choice
- 1/4 cup chopped almonds
- 1/4 cup shredded coconut
- 1 scoop chocolate or almond-flavored protein powder

Instructions:

1. In a blender, blend coconut milk, sugar, chopped almonds, shredded coconut, and protein powder until smooth.

2. Pour the mixture into the Ninja Creami Deluxe freezer attachment and churn until it thickens into gelato.

3. Serve the gelato immediately, garnished with extra chopped almonds and shredded coconut.

Nutritional Information per Serving:

- Calories: 250 kcal
- Protein: 8g
- Carbohydrates: 20g
- Fat: 18g
- Fiber: 2g

Pineapple Coconut Protein Gelato

- **Prep Time:** 15 minutes

- **Cook Time:** 0 minutes

- **Serving Size:** 4 servings

Ingredients:

- 2 cups frozen pineapple chunks

- 1 can (14 oz) coconut milk (full-fat)

- 1/2 cup granulated sugar or sweetener of choice

- 1 scoop vanilla or coconut-flavored protein powder

- Toasted coconut flakes for garnish

Instructions:

1. In a blender, blend frozen pineapple chunks, coconut milk, sugar, and protein powder until smooth.

2. Pour the mixture into the Ninja Creami Deluxe freezer attachment and churn until it reaches a gelato-like consistency.

3. Serve the gelato immediately, garnished with toasted coconut flakes.

Nutritional Information per Serving:

- Calories: 260 kcal

- Protein: 8g

- Carbohydrates: 30g

- Fat: 14g

- Fiber: 2g

Coffee Toffee Protein Gelato

- **Prep Time:** 20 minutes
- **Cook Time:** 0 minutes
- **Serving Size:** 4 servings

Ingredients:

- 1 cup heavy cream (or coconut cream)
- 1/2 cup granulated sugar or sweetener of choice
- 1/2 cup brewed coffee, cooled
- 1/4 cup toffee bits (sugar-free if preferred)
- 1 scoop vanilla or coffee-flavored protein powder

Instructions:

1. In a saucepan, combine the heavy cream, sugar, brewed coffee, toffee bits, and protein powder over medium heat, stirring until smooth.

2. Remove from heat and let it cool slightly.

3. Pour the mixture into the Ninja Creami Deluxe freezer attachment and churn until creamy.

4. Serve the gelato immediately for a soft texture or freeze for a firmer consistency.

Nutritional Information per Serving:

- Calories: 270 kcal
- Protein: 8g
- Carbohydrates: 25g
- Fat: 16g
- Fiber: 0g

Cherry Almond Protein Gelato

- **Prep Time:** 15 minutes

- **Cook Time:** 0 minutes

- **Serving Size:** 4 servings

Ingredients:

- 2 cups frozen cherries

- 1 cup heavy cream (or coconut cream)

- 1/2 cup granulated sugar or sweetener of choice

- 1/4 cup chopped almonds

- 1 scoop vanilla or almond-flavored protein powder

Instructions:

1. In a blender, blend frozen cherries, heavy cream, sugar, chopped almonds, and protein powder until smooth.

2. Pour the mixture into the Ninja Creami Deluxe freezer attachment and churn until it thickens into gelato.

3. Serve the gelato immediately or freeze for a firmer texture.

Nutritional Information per Serving:

- Calories: 260 kcal

- Protein: 8g

- Carbohydrates: 25g

- Fat: 16g

- Fiber: 2g

Chapter 4: Ice Cream Mix-Ins Recipes

Protein Peanut Butter Cups Mix-In

- **Prep Time:** 15 minutes

- **Cook Time:** 0 minutes

- **Serving Size:** 4 servings

Ingredients:

- 1/2 cup sugar-free chocolate chips

- 2 tablespoons coconut oil

- 1/4 cup natural peanut butter

- 1 scoop chocolate or vanilla protein powder

Instructions:

1. In a microwave-safe bowl, melt the sugar-free chocolate chips with coconut oil in 30-second intervals until smooth.

2. Line a mini muffin tin with paper liners.

3. Pour a small amount of melted chocolate into each liner, just enough to cover the bottom.

4. Place in the freezer for 5 minutes to set.

5. In a separate bowl, mix peanut butter and protein powder until well combined.

6. Spoon the peanut butter mixture on top of the chocolate in the muffin liners.

7. Pour the remaining melted chocolate over the peanut butter layer to cover.

8. Freeze for at least 30 minutes or until firm.

9. Remove from the muffin tin and chop into small pieces to mix into your ice cream.

Nutritional Information per Serving (1/4 of mix-ins):

- Calories: 120 kcal

- Protein: 7g

- Carbohydrates: 6g

- Fat: 10g

- Fiber: 2g

Protein Cookie Dough Chunks Mix-In

- **Prep Time:** 20 minutes

- **Cook Time:** 0 minutes

- **Serving Size:** 4 servings

Ingredients:

- 1/4 cup almond flour

- 2 tablespoons coconut flour

- 2 tablespoons sugar-free maple syrup

- 2 tablespoons almond butter

- 1 scoop vanilla or cookie dough-flavored protein powder

- Sugar-free chocolate chips (optional)

Instructions:

1. In a bowl, mix almond flour, coconut flour, sugar-free maple syrup, almond butter, and protein powder until a dough forms.

2. Fold in sugar-free chocolate chips if desired.

3. Roll the dough into small chunks and place them on a parchment-lined tray.

4. Freeze for at least 15 minutes or until firm.

5. Break the frozen cookie dough into chunks to mix into your ice cream.

Nutritional Information per Serving (1/4 of mix-ins):

- Calories: 110 kcal

- Protein: 6g

- Carbohydrates: 5g

- Fat: 8g

- Fiber: 2g

Protein Brownie Bites Mix-In

- **Prep Time:** 25 minutes

- **Cook Time:** 15 minutes

- **Serving Size:** 4 servings

Ingredients:

- 1/4 cup almond flour

- 2 tablespoons cocoa powder

- 1/4 teaspoon baking powder

- Pinch of salt

- 2 tablespoons sugar-free maple syrup

- 1 tablespoon coconut oil, melted

- 1 scoop chocolate protein powder

- Sugar-free chocolate chips (optional)

Instructions:

1. Preheat the oven to 350°F (175°C) and line a baking sheet with parchment paper.

2. In a bowl, mix almond flour, cocoa powder, baking powder, and salt.

3. Add sugar-free maple syrup, melted coconut oil, and chocolate protein powder. Mix until well combined.

4. Fold in sugar-free chocolate chips if desired.

5. Roll the dough into small balls and place them on the prepared baking sheet.

6. Bake for 12-15 minutes or until set.

7. Let the brownie bites cool completely, then chop them into chunks to mix into your ice cream.

Nutritional Information per Serving (1/4 of mix-ins):

- Calories: 110 kcal

- Protein: 7g

- Carbohydrates: 6g

- Fat: 7g

- Fiber: 2g

Protein Berry Swirl Mix-In

- **Prep Time:** 10 minutes

- **Cook Time:** 5 minutes

- **Serving Size:** 4 servings

Ingredients:

- 1 cup mixed berries (strawberries, blueberries, raspberries)

- 2 tablespoons water

- 1 tablespoon chia seeds

- 1 scoop vanilla or berry-flavored protein powder

Instructions:

1. In a saucepan, combine mixed berries and water. Cook over medium heat until the berries soften and release their juices, about 5 minutes.

2. Mash the berries with a fork or potato masher until smooth.

3. Stir in chia seeds and protein powder until well combined.

4. Let the berry mixture cool completely.

5. Swirl the berry mixture into your ice cream during the last few minutes of churning in the Ninja Creami Deluxe.

Nutritional Information per Serving (1/4 of mix-ins):

- Calories: 30 kcal

- Protein: 3g

- Carbohydrates: 4g

- Fat: 1g

- Fiber: 2g

Protein Almond Crunch Mix-In

- **Prep Time:** 15 minutes

- **Cook Time:** 10 minutes

- **Serving Size:** 4 servings

Ingredients:

- 1/4 cup almonds, chopped

- 2 tablespoons almond butter

- 1 tablespoon sugar-free maple syrup

- Pinch of salt

- 1 scoop vanilla or almond-flavored protein powder

Instructions:

1. In a skillet, toast chopped almonds over medium heat until lightly golden and fragrant, about 5 minutes.

2. In a bowl, mix almond butter, sugar-free maple syrup, salt, and protein powder until a thick paste forms.

3. Fold in the toasted almonds.

4. Spread the mixture onto a parchment-lined tray and freeze for 10 minutes or until firm.

5. Break the frozen almond crunch into small pieces to mix into your ice cream.

Nutritional Information per Serving (1/4 of mix-ins):

- Calories: 120 kcal

- Protein: 8g

- Carbohydrates: 5g

- Fat: 9g

- Fiber: 2g

Protein Salted Caramel Swirl Mix-In

- **Prep Time:** 10 minutes

- **Cook Time:** 10 minutes

- **Serving Size:** 4 servings

Ingredients:

- 1/2 cup sugar-free caramel sauce

- Pinch of sea salt

- 1 scoop vanilla or caramel-flavored protein powder

Instructions:

1. In a small bowl, mix the sugar-free caramel sauce with a pinch of sea salt until well combined.

2. Stir in the vanilla or caramel-flavored protein powder until smooth.

3. Pour the mixture into a small piping bag or zip-top bag.

4. Swirl the caramel mixture into your ice cream during the last few minutes of churning in the Ninja Creami Deluxe.

Nutritional Information per Serving (1/4 of mix-ins):

- Calories: 30 kcal

- Protein: 2g

- Carbohydrates: 6g

- Fat: 0g

- Fiber: 0g

Protein Oreo Cookie Crumble Mix-In

- **Prep Time:** 10 minutes

- **Cook Time:** 0 minutes

- **Serving Size:** 4 servings

Ingredients:

- 4 sugar-free Oreo cookies, crushed

- 1 scoop cookies and cream or chocolate-flavored protein powder

Instructions:

1. Crush the sugar-free Oreo cookies into small pieces.

2. In a bowl, mix the crushed cookies with the cookies and cream or chocolate-flavored protein powder until well combined.

3. Sprinkle the cookie crumble mixture into your ice cream during the last few minutes of churning in the Ninja Creami Deluxe.

Nutritional Information per Serving (1/4 of mix-ins):

- Calories: 60 kcal

- Protein: 4g

- Carbohydrates: 7g

- Fat: 2g

- Fiber: 1g

Protein Mint Chocolate Chip Mix-In

- **Prep Time:** 10 minutes

- **Cook Time:** 0 minutes

- **Serving Size:** 4 servings

Ingredients:

- 1/4 cup sugar-free chocolate chips

- 1/4 teaspoon peppermint extract

- 1 scoop chocolate or mint-flavored protein powder

Instructions:

1. Melt the sugar-free chocolate chips in a microwave-safe bowl in 30-second intervals until smooth.

2. Stir in the peppermint extract and chocolate or mint-flavored protein powder until well combined.

3. Let the mixture cool slightly.

4. Drop small clusters of the chocolate mixture into your ice cream during the last few minutes of churning in the Ninja Creami Deluxe.

Nutritional Information per Serving (1/4 of mix-ins):

- Calories: 70 kcal

- Protein: 5g

- Carbohydrates: 4g

- Fat: 4g

- Fiber: 1g

Protein Coconut Macaroon Mix-In

- **Prep Time:** 15 minutes

- **Cook Time:** 15 minutes

- **Serving Size:** 4 servings

Ingredients:

- 1/2 cup shredded coconut

- 2 tablespoons sugar-free maple syrup

- 1/4 teaspoon almond extract

- 1 scoop vanilla or coconut-flavored protein powder

Instructions:

1. Preheat the oven to 325°F (160°C) and line a baking sheet with parchment paper.

2. In a bowl, mix shredded coconut, sugar-free maple syrup, almond extract, and protein powder until well combined.

3. Form the mixture into small macaroon-shaped cookies and place them on the prepared baking sheet.

4. Bake for 12-15 minutes or until lightly golden.

5. Let the coconut macaroons cool completely, then break them into chunks to mix into your ice cream.

Nutritional Information per Serving (1/4 of mix-ins):

- Calories: 90 kcal

- Protein: 5g

- Carbohydrates: 6g

- Fat: 5g

- Fiber: 2g

Protein Mixed Nut Crunch Mix-In

- **Prep Time:** 15 minutes

- **Cook Time:** 10 minutes

- **Serving Size:** 4 servings

Ingredients:

- 1/4 cup mixed nuts (almonds, walnuts, cashews), chopped

- 2 tablespoons sugar-free maple syrup

- Pinch of salt

- 1 scoop vanilla or mixed nut-flavored protein powder

Instructions:

1. In a skillet, toast the chopped mixed nuts over medium heat until lightly golden and fragrant, about 5-7 minutes.

2. Drizzle sugar-free maple syrup over the nuts and sprinkle with a pinch of salt. Stir until the nuts are coated.

3. Transfer the nut mixture to a parchment-lined tray and let it cool completely.

4. Once cooled, break the nut clusters into smaller pieces to mix into your ice cream.

Nutritional Information per Serving (1/4 of mix-ins):

- Calories: 110 kcal

- Protein: 6g

- Carbohydrates: 6g

- Fat: 8g

- Fiber: 2g

Protein Cinnamon Roll Swirl Mix-In

- **Prep Time:** 10 minutes

- **Cook Time:** 0 minutes

- **Serving Size:** 4 servings

Ingredients:

- 2 tablespoons almond butter

- 2 tablespoons sugar-free maple syrup

- 1 teaspoon ground cinnamon

- 1 scoop vanilla or cinnamon roll-flavored protein powder

Instructions:

1. In a bowl, mix almond butter, sugar-free maple syrup, ground cinnamon, and protein powder until well combined.

2. Swirl the cinnamon mixture into your ice cream during the last few minutes of churning in the Ninja Creami Deluxe.

Nutritional Information per Serving (1/4 of mix-ins):

- Calories: 90 kcal

- Protein: 5g

- Carbohydrates: 6g

- Fat: 6g

- Fiber: 2g

Protein Chocolate Almond Crunch Mix-In

- **Prep Time:** 15 minutes
- **Cook Time:** 0 minutes
- **Serving Size:** 4 servings

Ingredients:

- 1/4 cup almonds, chopped
- 2 tablespoons sugar-free chocolate chips
- 1 scoop chocolate or almond-flavored protein powder

Instructions:

1. In a skillet, toast chopped almonds over medium heat until lightly golden and fragrant, about 5 minutes.
2. Melt sugar-free chocolate chips in a microwave-safe bowl in 30-second intervals until smooth.
3. In a separate bowl, mix toasted almonds and protein powder.
4. Pour the melted chocolate over the almond mixture and stir until well coated.
5. Spread the mixture onto a parchment-lined tray and freeze for 10 minutes or until firm.
6. Break the frozen chocolate almond crunch into chunks to mix into your ice cream.

Nutritional Information per Serving (1/4 of mix-ins):

- Calories: 100 kcal
- Protein: 6g
- Carbohydrates: 6g
- Fat: 7g
- Fiber: 2g

Protein Salted Pretzel Mix-In

- **Prep Time:** 5 minutes
- **Cook Time:** 0 minutes
- **Serving Size:** 4 servings

Ingredients:

- 1/2 cup mini salted pretzels, crushed
- 1 scoop vanilla or caramel-flavored protein powder

Instructions:

1. Crush the mini salted pretzels into small pieces.
2. In a bowl, mix the crushed pretzels with the vanilla or caramel-flavored protein powder until well combined.
3. Sprinkle the pretzel mixture into your ice cream during the last few minutes of churning in the Ninja Creami Deluxe.

Nutritional Information per Serving (1/4 of mix-ins):

- Calories: 60 kcal
- Protein: 5g
- Carbohydrates: 7g
- Fat: 1g
- Fiber: 1g

Protein Pumpkin Spice Swirl Mix-In

- **Prep Time:** 10 minutes

- **Cook Time:** 0 minutes

- **Serving Size:** 4 servings

Ingredients:

- 2 tablespoons pumpkin puree

- 1 tablespoon sugar-free maple syrup

- 1/2 teaspoon pumpkin pie spice

- 1 scoop vanilla or pumpkin spice-flavored protein powder

Instructions:

1. In a bowl, mix pumpkin puree, sugar-free maple syrup, pumpkin pie spice, and protein powder until well combined.

2. Swirl the pumpkin spice mixture into your ice cream during the last few minutes of churning in the Ninja Creami Deluxe.

Nutritional Information per Serving (1/4 of mix-ins):

- Calories: 40 kcal

- Protein: 3g

- Carbohydrates: 5g

- Fat: 1g

- Fiber: 1g

Protein Mocha Crunch Mix-In

- **Prep Time:** 15 minutes

- **Cook Time:** 0 minutes

- **Serving Size:** 4 servings

Ingredients:

- 1/4 cup roasted coffee beans, crushed

- 2 tablespoons sugar-free chocolate chips

- 1 scoop chocolate or mocha-flavored protein powder

Instructions:

1. Crush the roasted coffee beans into small pieces.

2. Melt sugar-free chocolate chips in a microwave-safe bowl in 30-second intervals until smooth.

3. In a bowl, mix the crushed coffee beans and protein powder.

4. Pour the melted chocolate over the coffee bean mixture and stir until well coated.

5. Spread the mixture onto a parchment-lined tray and freeze for 10 minutes or until firm.

6. Break the frozen mocha crunch into chunks to mix into your ice cream.

Nutritional Information per Serving (1/4 of mix-ins):

- Calories: 90 kcal

- Protein: 5g

- Carbohydrates: 7g

- Fat: 5g

- Fiber: 1g

Chapter 5: Milkshake and Lite Ice Cream Recipes

Vanilla Protein Milkshake

- **Prep Time:** 5 minutes

- **Cook Time:** 0 minutes

- **Serving Size:** 2 servings

Ingredients:

- 2 cups vanilla protein-fortified milk or almond milk

- 1 scoop vanilla protein powder

- 1/2 teaspoon vanilla extract

- Ice cubes (optional)

- Whipped cream for topping (optional)

- Sprinkle of cinnamon (optional)

Instructions:

1. In the Ninja Creami Deluxe blender pitcher, combine the vanilla protein-fortified milk, vanilla protein powder, and vanilla extract.

2. Add ice cubes if a thicker consistency is desired.

3. Blend until smooth and creamy.

4. Pour into glasses, top with whipped cream if desired, and sprinkle with cinnamon.

5. Serve immediately.

Nutritional Information per Serving:

- Calories: 150 kcal
- Protein: 20g
- Carbohydrates: 10g
- Fat: 3g

- Fiber: 1g

Chocolate Peanut Butter Protein Milkshake

- **Prep Time:** 5 minutes

- **Cook Time:** 0 minutes

- **Serving Size:** 2 servings

Ingredients:

- 2 cups chocolate protein-fortified milk or almond milk

- 1 scoop chocolate protein powder

- 2 tablespoons natural peanut butter

- Ice cubes (optional)

- Whipped cream for topping (optional)

- Drizzle of sugar-free chocolate syrup (optional)

Instructions:

1. In the Ninja Creami Deluxe blender pitcher, combine the chocolate protein-fortified milk, chocolate protein powder, and natural peanut butter.

2. Add ice cubes if desired for a thicker shake.

3. Blend until smooth and creamy.

4. Pour into glasses, top with whipped cream if desired, and drizzle with sugar-free chocolate syrup.

5. Serve immediately.

Nutritional Information per Serving:

- Calories: 220 kcal

- Protein: 25g

- Carbohydrates: 12g

- Fat: 8g

- Fiber: 2g

Strawberry Banana Protein Smoothie

- **Prep Time:** 5 minutes

- **Cook Time:** 0 minutes

- **Serving Size:** 2 servings

Ingredients:

- 1 cup frozen strawberries

- 1 ripe banana

- 2 cups strawberry protein-fortified milk or almond milk

- 1 scoop vanilla protein powder

- Ice cubes (optional)

- Fresh strawberries for garnish (optional)

Instructions:

1. In the Ninja Creami Deluxe blender pitcher, combine the frozen strawberries, ripe banana, strawberry protein-fortified milk, and vanilla protein powder.

2. Add ice cubes if desired for a colder smoothie.

3. Blend until smooth and creamy.

4. Pour into glasses, garnish with fresh strawberries if desired.

5. Serve immediately.

Nutritional Information per Serving:

- Calories: 180 kcal

- Protein: 20g

- Carbohydrates: 20g

- Fat: 2g

- Fiber: 5g

Coffee Protein Milkshake

- **Prep Time:** 5 minutes
- **Cook Time:** 0 minutes
- **Serving Size:** 2 servings

Ingredients:

- 1 cup chilled brewed coffee
- 1 cup chocolate protein-fortified milk or almond milk
- 1 scoop chocolate or vanilla protein powder
- Ice cubes (optional)
- Whipped cream for topping (optional)
- Sprinkle of cocoa powder (optional)

Instructions:

1. In the Ninja Creami Deluxe blender pitcher, combine the chilled brewed coffee, chocolate protein-fortified milk, and protein powder.
2. Add ice cubes if desired for a colder shake.
3. Blend until smooth and creamy.
4. Pour into glasses, top with whipped cream if desired, and sprinkle with cocoa powder.
5. Serve immediately.

Nutritional Information per Serving:

- Calories: 130 kcal
- Protein: 15g
- Carbohydrates: 10g
- Fat: 3g
- Fiber: 2g

Mint Chocolate Chip Protein Milkshake

- **Prep Time:** 5 minutes
- **Cook Time:** 0 minutes
- **Serving Size:** 2 servings

Ingredients:

- 2 cups mint chocolate chip protein-fortified milk or almond milk
- 1 scoop chocolate protein powder
- 1/4 teaspoon mint extract
- Ice cubes (optional)
- Whipped cream for topping (optional)
- Sugar-free chocolate chips (optional)

Instructions:

1. In the Ninja Creami Deluxe blender pitcher, combine the mint chocolate chip protein-fortified milk, chocolate protein powder, and mint extract.
2. Add ice cubes if desired for a colder shake.
3. Blend until smooth and creamy.
4. Pour into glasses, top with whipped cream if desired, and sprinkle with sugar-free chocolate chips.
5. Serve immediately.

Nutritional Information per Serving:

- Calories: 160 kcal
- Protein: 20g
- Carbohydrates: 10g
- Fat: 4g
- Fiber: 1g

Vanilla Protein Lite Ice Cream

- **Prep Time:** 10 minutes

- **Cook Time:** 0 minutes

- **Serving Size:** 4 servings

Ingredients:

- 2 cups Greek yogurt (plain or vanilla-flavored)

- 1/2 cup vanilla protein powder

- 2 tablespoons sugar-free sweetener (such as erythritol or stevia)

- 1 teaspoon vanilla extract

Instructions:

1. In a mixing bowl, combine Greek yogurt, vanilla protein powder, sugar-free sweetener, and vanilla extract.

2. Whisk until smooth and well combined.

3. Transfer the mixture to the Ninja Creami Deluxe freezer attachment and churn until it reaches a soft-serve consistency.

4. Serve immediately for a soft texture or transfer to a freezer-safe container and freeze for 1-2 hours for a firmer texture.

Nutritional Information per Serving:

- Calories: 120 kcal

- Protein: 15g

- Carbohydrates: 7g

- Fat: 3g

- Fiber: 0g

Strawberry Protein Lite Ice Cream

- **Prep Time:** 10 minutes
- **Cook Time:** 0 minutes
- **Serving Size:** 4 servings

Ingredients:

- 2 cups Greek yogurt (plain or strawberry-flavored)
- 1/2 cup strawberry protein powder
- 1 cup frozen strawberries, chopped
- 2 tablespoons sugar-free sweetener (such as erythritol or stevia)

Instructions:

1. In a mixing bowl, combine Greek yogurt, strawberry protein powder, frozen strawberries, and sugar-free sweetener.
2. Whisk until smooth and well combined.
3. Transfer the mixture to the Ninja Creami Deluxe freezer attachment and churn until it reaches a soft-serve consistency.
4. Serve immediately for a soft texture or transfer to a freezer-safe container and freeze for 1-2 hours for a firmer texture.

Nutritional Information per Serving:

- Calories: 140 kcal
- Protein: 17g
- Carbohydrates: 10g
- Fat: 2g
- Fiber: 2g

Coffee Protein Lite Ice Cream

- **Prep Time:** 10 minutes
- **Cook Time:** 0 minutes
- **Serving Size:** 4 servings

Ingredients:

- 2 cups Greek yogurt (plain or coffee-flavored)
- 1/2 cup coffee protein powder
- 1/2 cup chilled brewed coffee
- 2 tablespoons sugar-free sweetener (such as erythritol or stevia)

Instructions:

1. In a mixing bowl, combine Greek yogurt, coffee protein powder, chilled brewed coffee, and sugar-free sweetener.
2. Whisk until smooth and well combined.
3. Transfer the mixture to the Ninja Creami Deluxe freezer attachment and churn until it reaches a soft-serve consistency.
4. Serve immediately for a soft texture or transfer to a freezer-safe container and freeze for 1-2 hours for a firmer texture.

Nutritional Information per Serving:

- Calories: 120 kcal
- Protein: 15g
- Carbohydrates: 7g
- Fat: 2g
- Fiber: 0g

Chocolate Chip Cookie Dough Protein Lite Ice Cream

- **Prep Time:** 15 minutes
- **Cook Time:** 0 minutes
- **Serving Size:** 4 servings

Ingredients:

- 2 cups Greek yogurt (plain or vanilla-flavored)
- 1/2 cup vanilla protein powder
- 1/4 cup sugar-free chocolate chips
- 1/4 cup almond flour
- 2 tablespoons sugar-free sweetener (such as erythritol or stevia)
- 1/2 teaspoon vanilla extract

Instructions:

1. In a mixing bowl, combine Greek yogurt, vanilla protein powder, sugar-free sweetener, and vanilla extract.

2. Fold in sugar-free chocolate chips and almond flour until well distributed.

3. Transfer the mixture to the Ninja Creami Deluxe freezer attachment and churn until it reaches a soft-serve consistency.

4. Serve immediately for a soft texture or transfer to a freezer-safe container and freeze for 1-2 hours for a firmer texture.

Nutritional Information per Serving:

- Calories: 150 kcal
- Protein: 18g
- Carbohydrates: 10g
- Fat: 5g
- Fiber: 2g

Banana Protein Lite Ice Cream

- **Prep Time:** 10 minutes

- **Cook Time:** 0 minutes

- **Serving Size:** 4 servings

Ingredients:

- 2 cups Greek yogurt (plain or banana-flavored)

- 1/2 cup banana protein powder

- 1 ripe banana, mashed

- 2 tablespoons sugar-free sweetener (such as erythritol or stevia)

Instructions:

1. In a mixing bowl, combine Greek yogurt, banana protein powder, mashed ripe banana, and sugar-free sweetener.

2. Whisk until smooth and well combined.

3. Transfer the mixture to the Ninja Creami Deluxe freezer attachment and churn until it reaches a soft-serve consistency.

4. Serve immediately for a soft texture or transfer to a freezer-safe container and freeze for 1-2 hours for a firmer texture.

Nutritional Information per Serving:

- Calories: 140 kcal

- Protein: 16g

- Carbohydrates: 15g

- Fat: 2g

- Fiber: 2g

Blueberry Protein Lite Ice Cream

- **Prep Time:** 10 minutes

- **Cook Time:** 0 minutes

- **Serving Size:** 4 servings

Ingredients:

- 2 cups Greek yogurt (plain or blueberry-flavored)

- 1/2 cup blueberry protein powder

- 1 cup frozen blueberries

- 2 tablespoons sugar-free sweetener (such as erythritol or stevia)

Instructions:

1. In a mixing bowl, combine Greek yogurt, blueberry protein powder, frozen blueberries, and sugar-free sweetener.

2. Whisk until smooth and well combined.

3. Transfer the mixture to the Ninja Creami Deluxe freezer attachment and churn until it reaches a soft-serve consistency.

4. Serve immediately for a soft texture or transfer to a freezer-safe container and freeze for 1-2 hours for a firmer texture.

Nutritional Information per Serving:

- Calories: 150 kcal

- Protein: 17g

- Carbohydrates: 20g

- Fat: 2g

- Fiber: 4g

Chocolate Raspberry Protein Milkshake

- **Prep Time:** 5 minutes

- **Cook Time:** 0 minutes

- **Serving Size:** 2 servings

Ingredients:

- 2 cups chocolate protein-fortified milk or almond milk

- 1 scoop chocolate protein powder

- 1/2 cup fresh or frozen raspberries

- Ice cubes (optional)

- Whipped cream for topping (optional)

- Fresh raspberries for garnish (optional)

Instructions:

1. In the Ninja Creami Deluxe blender pitcher, combine the chocolate protein-fortified milk, chocolate protein powder, and raspberries.

2. Add ice cubes if desired for a colder shake.

3. Blend until smooth and creamy.

4. Pour into glasses, top with whipped cream if desired, and garnish with fresh raspberries.

5. Serve immediately.

Nutritional Information per Serving:

- Calories: 180 kcal

- Protein: 20g

- Carbohydrates: 12g

- Fat: 3g

- Fiber: 4g

Protein-Packed Coffee Shake

- **Prep Time:** 5 minutes
- **Cook Time:** 0 minutes
- **Serving Size:** 2 servings

Ingredients:

- 1 cup chilled brewed coffee
- 1 cup chocolate protein-fortified milk or almond milk
- 1 scoop vanilla or chocolate protein powder
- Ice cubes (optional)
- Whipped cream for topping (optional)
- Cocoa powder for dusting (optional)

Instructions:

1. In the Ninja Creami Deluxe blender pitcher, combine the chilled brewed coffee, chocolate protein-fortified milk, and protein powder.
2. Add ice cubes if desired for a colder shake.
3. Blend until smooth and creamy.
4. Pour into glasses, top with whipped cream if desired, and dust with cocoa powder.
5. Serve immediately.

Nutritional Information per Serving:

- Calories: 130 kcal
- Protein: 15g
- Carbohydrates: 10g
- Fat: 3g
- Fiber: 1g

Peanut Butter Banana Protein Shake

- **Prep Time:** 5 minutes
- **Cook Time:** 0 minutes
- **Serving Size:** 2 servings

Ingredients:

- 2 cups vanilla protein-fortified milk or almond milk
- 1 scoop vanilla protein powder
- 2 tablespoons natural peanut butter
- 1 ripe banana
- Ice cubes (optional)
- Whipped cream for topping (optional)
- Sliced bananas for garnish (optional)

Instructions:

1. In the Ninja Creami Deluxe blender pitcher, combine the vanilla protein-fortified milk, vanilla protein powder, natural peanut butter, and ripe banana.
2. Add ice cubes if desired for a colder shake.
3. Blend until smooth and creamy.
4. Pour into glasses, top with whipped cream if desired, and garnish with sliced bananas.
5. Serve immediately.

Nutritional Information per Serving:

- Calories: 220 kcal
- Protein: 25g
- Carbohydrates: 15g
- Fat: 8g
- Fiber: 2g

Chapter 6: Sorbet Recipes

Mango Protein Sorbet

- **Prep Time:** 10 minutes

- **Freeze Time:** 4 hours

- **Serving Size:** 4 servings

Ingredients:

- 2 cups frozen mango chunks

- 1 scoop vanilla or mango-flavored protein powder

- 1/4 cup water or coconut water

- 1 tablespoon honey or agave syrup (optional)

Instructions:

1. Add the frozen mango chunks, protein powder, water, and optional honey/agave syrup to the Ninja Creami Deluxe blender pitcher.

2. Blend until smooth and creamy.

3. Transfer the mixture to a freezer-safe container and freeze for at least 4 hours or until firm.

4. Scoop and serve the mango protein sorbet.

Nutritional Information per Serving:

- Calories: 90 kcal

- Protein: 5g

- Carbohydrates: 20g

- Fat: 0g

- Fiber: 2g

Strawberry Protein Sorbet

- **Prep Time:** 10 minutes

- **Freeze Time:** 4 hours

- **Serving Size:** 4 servings

Ingredients:

- 2 cups frozen strawberries

- 1 scoop vanilla or strawberry-flavored protein powder

- 1/4 cup water or almond milk

- 1 tablespoon honey or maple syrup (optional)

Instructions:

1. In the Ninja Creami Deluxe blender pitcher, combine the frozen strawberries, protein powder, water or almond milk, and optional honey/maple syrup.

2. Blend until smooth and creamy.

3. Transfer the mixture to a freezer-safe container and freeze for at least 4 hours or until firm.

4. Scoop and serve the strawberry protein sorbet.

Nutritional Information per Serving:

- Calories: 80 kcal

- Protein: 4g

- Carbohydrates: 18g

- Fat: 0g

- Fiber: 3g

Blueberry Protein Sorbet

- **Prep Time:** 10 minutes

- **Freeze Time:** 4 hours

- **Serving Size:** 4 servings

Ingredients:

- 2 cups frozen blueberries

- 1 scoop vanilla or blueberry-flavored protein powder

- 1/4 cup water or coconut water

- 1 tablespoon honey or agave syrup (optional)

Instructions:

1. Combine frozen blueberries, protein powder, water or coconut water, and optional honey/agave syrup in the Ninja Creami Deluxe blender pitcher.

2. Blend until smooth and creamy.

3. Transfer the mixture to a freezer-safe container and freeze for at least 4 hours or until firm.

4. Scoop and serve the blueberry protein sorbet.

Nutritional Information per Serving:

- Calories: 70 kcal

- Protein: 3g

- Carbohydrates: 16g

- Fat: 0g

- Fiber: 4g

Raspberry Protein Sorbet

- **Prep Time:** 10 minutes
- **Freeze Time:** 4 hours
- **Serving Size:** 4 servings

Ingredients:

- 2 cups frozen raspberries
- 1 scoop vanilla or raspberry-flavored protein powder
- 1/4 cup water or almond milk
- 1 tablespoon honey or maple syrup (optional)

Instructions:

1. In the Ninja Creami Deluxe blender pitcher, combine the frozen raspberries, protein powder, water or almond milk, and optional honey/maple syrup.
2. Blend until smooth and creamy.
3. Transfer the mixture to a freezer-safe container and freeze for at least 4 hours or until firm.
4. Scoop and serve the raspberry protein sorbet.

Nutritional Information per Serving:

- Calories: 80 kcal
- Protein: 4g
- Carbohydrates: 18g
- Fat: 0g
- Fiber: 5g

Pineapple Coconut Protein Sorbet

- **Prep Time:** 10 minutes

- **Freeze Time:** 4 hours

- **Serving Size:** 4 servings

Ingredients:

- 2 cups frozen pineapple chunks

- 1 scoop vanilla or coconut-flavored protein powder

- 1/4 cup coconut milk

- 1 tablespoon honey or agave syrup (optional)

Instructions:

1. Combine frozen pineapple chunks, protein powder, coconut milk, and optional honey/agave syrup in the Ninja Creami Deluxe blender pitcher.

2. Blend until smooth and creamy.

3. Transfer the mixture to a freezer-safe container and freeze for at least 4 hours or until firm.

4. Scoop and serve the pineapple coconut protein sorbet.

Nutritional Information per Serving:

- Calories: 100 kcal

- Protein: 4g

- Carbohydrates: 20g

- Fat: 2g

- Fiber: 2g

Kiwi Lime Protein Sorbet

- **Prep Time:** 10 minutes
- **Freeze Time:** 4 hours
- **Serving Size:** 4 servings

Ingredients:

- 2 cups frozen kiwi chunks
- Juice of 2 limes
- Zest of 1 lime
- 1 scoop vanilla or lime-flavored protein powder
- 1/4 cup water or coconut water
- 1 tablespoon honey or agave syrup (optional)

Instructions:

1. In the Ninja Creami Deluxe blender pitcher, combine the frozen kiwi chunks, lime juice, lime zest, protein powder, water or coconut water, and optional honey/agave syrup.
2. Blend until smooth and creamy.
3. Transfer the mixture to a freezer-safe container and freeze for at least 4 hours or until firm.
4. Scoop and serve the kiwi lime protein sorbet.

Nutritional Information per Serving:

- Calories: 90 kcal
- Protein: 3g
- Carbohydrates: 20g
- Fat: 0g
- Fiber: 3g

Lemon Protein Sorbet

- **Prep Time:** 10 minutes

- **Freeze Time:** 4 hours

- **Serving Size:** 4 servings

Ingredients:

- Juice of 4 lemons

- Zest of 1 lemon

- 1 scoop vanilla or lemon-flavored protein powder

- 1/4 cup water or coconut water

- 1 tablespoon honey or agave syrup (optional)

Instructions:

1. Combine lemon juice, lemon zest, protein powder, water or coconut water, and optional honey/agave syrup in the Ninja Creami Deluxe blender pitcher.

2. Blend until smooth and creamy.

3. Transfer the mixture to a freezer-safe container and freeze for at least 4 hours or until firm.

4. Scoop and serve the lemon protein sorbet.

Nutritional Information per Serving:

- Calories: 80 kcal

- Protein: 3g

- Carbohydrates: 18g

- Fat: 0g

- Fiber: 2g

Watermelon Mint Protein Sorbet

- **Prep Time:** 10 minutes

- **Freeze Time:** 4 hours

- **Serving Size:** 4 servings

Ingredients:

- 2 cups frozen watermelon cubes

- 1 scoop vanilla or watermelon-flavored protein powder

- Juice of 1 lime

- Fresh mint leaves, chopped

- 1/4 cup water or coconut water

- 1 tablespoon honey or agave syrup (optional)

Instructions:

1. In the Ninja Creami Deluxe blender pitcher, combine the frozen watermelon cubes, protein powder, lime juice, chopped mint leaves, water or coconut water, and optional honey/agave syrup.

2. Blend until smooth and creamy.

3. Transfer the mixture to a freezer-safe container and freeze for at least 4 hours or until firm.

4. Scoop and serve the watermelon mint protein sorbet.

Nutritional Information per Serving:

- Calories: 70 kcal

- Protein: 3g

- Carbohydrates: 15g

- Fat: 0g

- Fiber: 1g

Peach Protein Sorbet

- **Prep Time:** 10 minutes
- **Freeze Time:** 4 hours
- **Serving Size:** 4 servings

Ingredients:

- 2 cups frozen peach slices
- 1 scoop vanilla or peach-flavored protein powder
- 1/4 cup water or almond milk
- 1 tablespoon honey or agave syrup (optional)

Instructions:

1. In the Ninja Creami Deluxe blender pitcher, combine the frozen peach slices, protein powder, water or almond milk, and optional honey/agave syrup.

2. Blend until smooth and creamy.

3. Transfer the mixture to a freezer-safe container and freeze for at least 4 hours or until firm.

4. Scoop and serve the peach protein sorbet.

Nutritional Information per Serving:

- Calories: 80 kcal
- Protein: 4g
- Carbohydrates: 18g
- Fat: 0g
- Fiber: 2g

Mixed Berry Protein Sorbet

- **Prep Time:** 10 minutes

- **Freeze Time:** 4 hours

- **Serving Size:** 4 servings

Ingredients:

- 1 cup frozen strawberries

- 1 cup frozen blueberries

- 1 scoop vanilla or mixed berry-flavored protein powder

- 1/4 cup water or coconut water

- 1 tablespoon honey or agave syrup (optional)

Instructions:

1. In the Ninja Creami Deluxe blender pitcher, combine the frozen strawberries, frozen blueberries, protein powder, water or coconut water, and optional honey/agave syrup.

2. Blend until smooth and creamy.

3. Transfer the mixture to a freezer-safe container and freeze for at least 4 hours or until firm.

4. Scoop and serve the mixed berry protein sorbet.

Nutritional Information per Serving:

- Calories: 90 kcal

- Protein: 3g

- Carbohydrates: 22g

- Fat: 0g

- Fiber: 4g

Pineapple Mango Protein Sorbet

- **Prep Time:** 10 minutes
- **Freeze Time:** 4 hours
- **Serving Size:** 4 servings

Ingredients:

- 1 cup frozen pineapple chunks
- 1 cup frozen mango chunks
- 1 scoop vanilla or tropical fruit-flavored protein powder
- 1/4 cup coconut milk
- 1 tablespoon honey or agave syrup (optional)

Instructions:

1. In the Ninja Creami Deluxe blender pitcher, combine the frozen pineapple chunks, frozen mango chunks, protein powder, coconut milk, and optional honey/agave syrup.
2. Blend until smooth and creamy.
3. Transfer the mixture to a freezer-safe container and freeze for at least 4 hours or until firm.
4. Scoop and serve the pineapple mango protein sorbet.

Nutritional Information per Serving:

- Calories: 110 kcal
- Protein: 4g
- Carbohydrates: 24g
- Fat: 1g
- Fiber: 3g

Apple Cinnamon Protein Sorbet

- **Prep Time:** 10 minutes

- **Freeze Time:** 4 hours

- **Serving Size:** 4 servings

Ingredients:

- 2 cups frozen apple slices

- 1 scoop vanilla or apple-cinnamon-flavored protein powder

- 1/4 cup almond milk or apple juice

- 1/2 teaspoon ground cinnamon

- 1 tablespoon honey or agave syrup (optional)

Instructions:

1. In the Ninja Creami Deluxe blender pitcher, combine the frozen apple slices, protein powder, almond milk or apple juice, ground cinnamon, and optional honey/agave syrup.

2. Blend until smooth and creamy.

3. Transfer the mixture to a freezer-safe container and freeze for at least 4 hours or until firm.

4. Scoop and serve the apple cinnamon protein sorbet.

Nutritional Information per Serving:

- Calories: 90 kcal

- Protein: 3g

- Carbohydrates: 20g

- Fat: 0g

- Fiber: 3g

Avocado Lime Protein Sorbet

- **Prep Time:** 10 minutes

- **Freeze Time:** 4 hours

- **Serving Size:** 4 servings

Ingredients:

- 1 ripe avocado, peeled and pitted

- Juice of 2 limes

- Zest of 1 lime

- 1 scoop vanilla or lime-flavored protein powder

- 1/4 cup coconut water

- 1 tablespoon honey or agave syrup (optional)

Instructions:

1. In the Ninja Creami Deluxe blender pitcher, combine the ripe avocado, lime juice, lime zest, protein powder, coconut water, and optional honey/agave syrup.

2. Blend until smooth and creamy.

3. Transfer the mixture to a freezer-safe container and freeze for at least 4 hours or until firm.

4. Scoop and serve the avocado lime protein sorbet.

Nutritional Information per Serving:

- Calories: 120 kcal

- Protein: 5g

- Carbohydrates: 10g

- Fat: 7g

- Fiber: 5g

Cherry Vanilla Protein Sorbet

- **Prep Time:** 10 minutes

- **Freeze Time:** 4 hours

- **Serving Size:** 4 servings

Ingredients:

- 2 cups frozen cherries, pitted

- 1 scoop vanilla or cherry-flavored protein powder

- 1/4 cup water or almond milk

- 1 tablespoon honey or agave syrup (optional)

Instructions:

1. In the Ninja Creami Deluxe blender pitcher, combine the frozen cherries, protein powder, water or almond milk, and optional honey/agave syrup.

2. Blend until smooth and creamy.

3. Transfer the mixture to a freezer-safe container and freeze for at least 4 hours or until firm.

4. Scoop and serve the cherry vanilla protein sorbet.

Nutritional Information per Serving:

- Calories: 90 kcal

- Protein: 3g

- Carbohydrates: 20g

- Fat: 0g

- Fiber: 3g

Matcha Green Tea Protein Sorbet

- **Prep Time:** 10 minutes

- **Freeze Time:** 4 hours

- **Serving Size:** 4 servings

Ingredients:

- 2 teaspoons matcha green tea powder

- 1 scoop vanilla or green tea-flavored protein powder

- 1/4 cup coconut milk

- 1/4 cup water

- 1 tablespoon honey or agave syrup (optional)

Instructions:

1. In the Ninja Creami Deluxe blender pitcher, combine the matcha green tea powder, protein powder, coconut milk, water, and optional honey/agave syrup.

2. Blend until smooth and creamy.

3. Transfer the mixture to a freezer-safe container and freeze for at least 4 hours or until firm.

4. Scoop and serve the matcha green tea protein sorbet.

Nutritional Information per Serving:

- Calories: 100 kcal

- Protein: 4g

- Carbohydrates: 15g

- Fat: 3g

- Fiber: 2g

Pomegranate Berry Protein Sorbet

- **Prep Time:** 10 minutes

- **Freeze Time:** 4 hours

- **Serving Size:** 4 servings

Ingredients:

- 1 cup frozen pomegranate seeds

- 1/2 cup frozen mixed berries (such as raspberries, blackberries, and blueberries)

- 1 scoop vanilla or berry-flavored protein powder

- 1/4 cup water or pomegranate juice

- 1 tablespoon honey or agave syrup (optional)

Instructions:

1. In the Ninja Creami Deluxe blender pitcher, combine the frozen pomegranate seeds, mixed berries, protein powder, water or pomegranate juice, and optional honey/agave syrup.

2. Blend until smooth and creamy.

3. Transfer the mixture to a freezer-safe container and freeze for at least 4 hours or until firm.

4. Scoop and serve the pomegranate berry protein sorbet.

Nutritional Information per Serving:

- Calories: 110 kcal

- Protein: 4g

- Carbohydrates: 25g

- Fat: 1g

- Fiber: 5g

Pineapple Basil Protein Sorbet

- **Prep Time:** 10 minutes

- **Freeze Time:** 4 hours

- **Serving Size:** 4 servings

Ingredients:

- 2 cups frozen pineapple chunks

- Handful of fresh basil leaves

- 1 scoop vanilla or pineapple-flavored protein powder

- 1/4 cup coconut water

- 1 tablespoon honey or agave syrup (optional)

Instructions:

1. In the Ninja Creami Deluxe blender pitcher, combine the frozen pineapple chunks, fresh basil leaves, protein powder, coconut water, and optional honey/agave syrup.

2. Blend until smooth and creamy.

3. Transfer the mixture to a freezer-safe container and freeze for at least 4 hours or until firm.

4. Scoop and serve the pineapple basil protein sorbet.

Nutritional Information per Serving:

- Calories: 100 kcal

- Protein: 3g

- Carbohydrates: 22g

- Fat: 0g

- Fiber: 3g

Chapter 7: Smoothie Bowls Recipes

Mixed Berry Protein Smoothie Bowl

- **Prep Time:** 5 minutes
- **Serving Size:** 1 bowl

Ingredients:

- 1 cup frozen mixed berries (strawberries, blueberries, raspberries)
- 1 banana, frozen
- 1 scoop vanilla protein powder
- 1/2 cup almond milk or Greek yogurt
- Toppings: sliced fresh fruits, granola, chia seeds, shredded coconut

Instructions:

1. In the Ninja Creami Deluxe blender pitcher, combine the frozen mixed berries, frozen banana, vanilla protein powder, and almond milk or Greek yogurt.
2. Blend until smooth and creamy.
3. Pour the smoothie into a bowl.
4. Top with sliced fresh fruits, granola, chia seeds, and shredded coconut.
5. Enjoy immediately.

Nutritional Information:

- Calories: 350 kcal
- Protein: 25g
- Carbohydrates: 50g
- Fat: 7g
- Fiber: 10g

Tropical Mango Protein Smoothie Bowl

- **Prep Time:** 5 minutes
- **Serving Size:** 1 bowl

Ingredients:

- 1 cup frozen mango chunks
- 1/2 banana, frozen
- 1 scoop mango-flavored protein powder
- 1/2 cup coconut milk or pineapple juice
- Toppings: sliced fresh mango, pineapple chunks, coconut flakes, hemp seeds

Instructions:

1. Blend the frozen mango chunks, frozen banana, mango protein powder, and coconut milk or pineapple juice in the Ninja Creami Deluxe blender pitcher until smooth.
2. Pour the smoothie into a bowl.
3. Top with sliced fresh mango, pineapple chunks, coconut flakes, and hemp seeds.
4. Serve and enjoy immediately.

Nutritional Information:

- Calories: 380 kcal
- Protein: 30g
- Carbohydrates: 45g
- Fat: 10g
- Fiber: 8g

Green Goddess Protein Smoothie Bowl

- **Prep Time:** 5 minutes
- **Serving Size:** 1 bowl

Ingredients:

- 1 cup fresh spinach leaves
- 1/2 avocado
- 1/2 cup frozen pineapple chunks
- 1 scoop vanilla protein powder
- 1/2 cup almond milk or coconut water
- Toppings: sliced banana, kiwi slices, pumpkin seeds, honey drizzle

Instructions:

1. Blend the fresh spinach leaves, avocado, frozen pineapple chunks, vanilla protein powder, and almond milk or coconut water in the Ninja Creami Deluxe blender pitcher until smooth.
2. Pour the smoothie into a bowl.
3. Top with sliced banana, kiwi slices, pumpkin seeds, and a drizzle of honey.
4. Serve immediately.

Nutritional Information:

- Calories: 400 kcal
- Protein: 28g
- Carbohydrates: 45g
- Fat: 15g
- Fiber: 12g

Chocolate Peanut Butter Protein Smoothie Bowl

- **Prep Time:** 5 minutes

- **Serving Size:** 1 bowl

Ingredients:

- 1 banana, frozen

- 2 tablespoons unsweetened cocoa powder

- 1 scoop chocolate protein powder

- 1 tablespoon natural peanut butter

- 1/2 cup almond milk or soy milk

- Toppings: sliced banana, chopped peanuts, dark chocolate shavings, drizzle of peanut butter

Instructions:

1. Blend the frozen banana, cocoa powder, chocolate protein powder, natural peanut butter, and almond milk or soy milk in the Ninja Creami Deluxe blender pitcher until smooth.

2. Pour the smoothie into a bowl.

3. Top with sliced banana, chopped peanuts, dark chocolate shavings, and a drizzle of peanut butter.

4. Serve immediately.

Nutritional Information:

- Calories: 420 kcal

- Protein: 30g

- Carbohydrates: 50g

- Fat: 15g

- Fiber: 10g

Acai Berry Protein Smoothie Bowl

- **Prep Time:** 5 minutes

- **Serving Size:** 1 bowl

Ingredients:

- 1 packet frozen acai puree

- 1/2 banana, frozen

- 1 scoop vanilla or acai-flavored protein powder

- 1/2 cup almond milk or coconut water

- Toppings: granola, sliced strawberries, blueberries, chia seeds

Instructions:

1. Blend the frozen acai puree, frozen banana, vanilla or acai-flavored protein powder, and almond milk or coconut water in the Ninja Creami Deluxe blender pitcher until smooth.

2. Pour the smoothie into a bowl.

3. Top with granola, sliced strawberries, blueberries, and chia seeds.

4. Serve immediately.

Nutritional Information:

- Calories: 380 kcal

- Protein: 25g

- Carbohydrates: 50g

- Fat: 10g

- Fiber: 12g

Peach Raspberry Protein Smoothie Bowl

- **Prep Time:** 5 minutes
- **Serving Size:** 1 bowl

Ingredients:

- 1 cup frozen peaches
- 1/2 cup frozen raspberries
- 1 scoop vanilla or raspberry-flavored protein powder
- 1/2 cup almond milk or Greek yogurt
- Toppings: fresh peach slices, raspberries, almonds, honey drizzle

Instructions:

1. Blend the frozen peaches, frozen raspberries, vanilla or raspberry-flavored protein powder, and almond milk or Greek yogurt in the Ninja Creami Deluxe blender pitcher until smooth.
2. Pour the smoothie into a bowl.
3. Top with fresh peach slices, raspberries, almonds, and a drizzle of honey.
4. Serve immediately.

Nutritional Information:

- Calories: 340 kcal
- Protein: 30g
- Carbohydrates: 45g
- Fat: 8g
- Fiber: 10g

Coconut Pineapple Protein Smoothie Bowl

- **Prep Time:** 5 minutes

- **Serving Size:** 1 bowl

Ingredients:

- 1 cup frozen pineapple chunks

- 1/2 banana, frozen

- 1 scoop coconut or pineapple-flavored protein powder

- 1/2 cup coconut milk or pineapple juice

- Toppings: toasted coconut flakes, sliced banana, chia seeds, kiwi slices

Instructions:

1. Blend the frozen pineapple chunks, frozen banana, coconut or pineapple-flavored protein powder, and coconut milk or pineapple juice in the Ninja Creami Deluxe blender pitcher until smooth.

2. Pour the smoothie into a bowl.

3. Top with toasted coconut flakes, sliced banana, chia seeds, and kiwi slices.

4. Serve immediately.

Nutritional Information:

- Calories: 380 kcal

- Protein: 25g

- Carbohydrates: 45g

- Fat: 12g

- Fiber: 8g

Blueberry Almond Protein Smoothie Bowl

- **Prep Time:** 5 minutes

- **Serving Size:** 1 bowl

Ingredients:

- 1 cup frozen blueberries

- 1/2 banana, frozen

- 1 scoop vanilla or almond-flavored protein powder

- 1/2 cup almond milk or Greek yogurt

- Toppings: fresh blueberries, sliced almonds, almond butter drizzle, chia seeds

Instructions:

1. Blend the frozen blueberries, frozen banana, vanilla or almond-flavored protein powder, and almond milk or Greek yogurt in the Ninja Creami Deluxe blender pitcher until smooth.

2. Pour the smoothie into a bowl.

3. Top with fresh blueberries, sliced almonds, a drizzle of almond butter, and chia seeds.

4. Serve immediately.

Nutritional Information:

- Calories: 350 kcal

- Protein: 28g

- Carbohydrates: 45g

- Fat: 10g

- Fiber: 10g

Banana Chocolate Chip Protein Smoothie Bowl

- **Prep Time:** 5 minutes
- **Serving Size:** 1 bowl

Ingredients:

- 1 banana, frozen
- 1 tablespoon unsweetened cocoa powder
- 1 scoop chocolate protein powder
- 1/2 cup almond milk or soy milk
- Toppings: banana slices, dark chocolate chips, crushed almonds, honey drizzle

Instructions:

1. Blend the frozen banana, cocoa powder, chocolate protein powder, and almond milk or soy milk in the Ninja Creami Deluxe blender pitcher until smooth.
2. Pour the smoothie into a bowl.
3. Top with banana slices, dark chocolate chips, crushed almonds, and a drizzle of honey.
4. Serve immediately.

Nutritional Information:

- Calories: 380 kcal
- Protein: 30g
- Carbohydrates: 45g
- Fat: 12g
- Fiber: 8g

Cherry Chocolate Protein Smoothie Bowl

- **Prep Time:** 5 minutes

- **Serving Size:** 1 bowl

Ingredients:

- 1 cup frozen cherries, pitted

- 1 scoop chocolate protein powder

- 1/2 cup almond milk or Greek yogurt

- Toppings: fresh cherries, dark chocolate shavings, sliced almonds, honey drizzle

Instructions:

1. Blend the frozen cherries, chocolate protein powder, and almond milk or Greek yogurt in the Ninja Creami Deluxe blender pitcher until smooth.

2. Pour the smoothie into a bowl.

3. Top with fresh cherries, dark chocolate shavings, sliced almonds, and a drizzle of honey.

4. Serve immediately.

Nutritional Information:

- Calories: 320 kcal

- Protein: 25g

- Carbohydrates: 40g

- Fat: 8g

- Fiber: 8g

Pumpkin Spice Protein Smoothie Bowl

- **Prep Time:** 5 minutes

- **Serving Size:** 1 bowl

Ingredients:

- 1/2 cup pumpkin puree (canned or homemade)

- 1/2 banana, frozen

- 1 scoop vanilla or pumpkin spice-flavored protein powder

- 1/2 cup almond milk or coconut milk

- Toppings: pumpkin seeds, cinnamon, nutmeg, maple syrup drizzle

Instructions:

1. Blend the pumpkin puree, frozen banana, vanilla or pumpkin spice-flavored protein powder, and almond milk or coconut milk in the Ninja Creami Deluxe blender pitcher until smooth.

2. Pour the smoothie into a bowl.

3. Top with pumpkin seeds, a sprinkle of cinnamon and nutmeg, and a drizzle of maple syrup.

4. Serve immediately.

Nutritional Information:

- Calories: 330 kcal

- Protein: 25g

- Carbohydrates: 40g

- Fat: 10g

- Fiber: 8g

Mango Coconut Protein Smoothie Bowl

- **Prep Time:** 5 minutes
- **Serving Size:** 1 bowl

Ingredients:

- 1 cup frozen mango chunks
- 1/2 banana, frozen
- 1 scoop vanilla or coconut-flavored protein powder
- 1/2 cup coconut milk or almond milk
- Toppings: fresh mango slices, shredded coconut, granola, chia seeds

Instructions:

1. Blend the frozen mango chunks, frozen banana, vanilla or coconut-flavored protein powder, and coconut milk or almond milk in the Ninja Creami Deluxe blender pitcher until smooth.
2. Pour the smoothie into a bowl.
3. Top with fresh mango slices, shredded coconut, granola, and chia seeds.
4. Serve immediately.

Nutritional Information:

- Calories: 370 kcal
- Protein: 28g
- Carbohydrates: 45g
- Fat: 12g
- Fiber: 8g

Apple Cinnamon Protein Smoothie Bowl

- **Prep Time:** 5 minutes

- **Serving Size:** 1 bowl

Ingredients:

- 1 apple, peeled and chopped

- 1/2 banana, frozen

- 1 scoop vanilla or cinnamon-flavored protein powder

- 1/2 cup almond milk or apple juice

- Toppings: sliced apple, cinnamon powder, granola, walnuts

Instructions:

1. Blend the chopped apple, frozen banana, vanilla or cinnamon-flavored protein powder, and almond milk or apple juice in the Ninja Creami Deluxe blender pitcher until smooth.

2. Pour the smoothie into a bowl.

3. Top with sliced apple, a sprinkle of cinnamon powder, granola, and walnuts.

4. Serve immediately.

Nutritional Information:

- Calories: 320 kcal

- Protein: 25g

- Carbohydrates: 40g

- Fat: 8g

- Fiber: 6g

Peanut Butter Banana Protein Smoothie Bowl

- **Prep Time:** 5 minutes
- **Serving Size:** 1 bowl

Ingredients:

- 1 banana, frozen
- 2 tablespoons natural peanut butter
- 1 scoop vanilla or peanut butter-flavored protein powder
- 1/2 cup almond milk or soy milk
- Toppings: sliced banana, peanut butter drizzle, chopped peanuts, chocolate chips

Instructions:

1. Blend the frozen banana, natural peanut butter, vanilla or peanut butter-flavored protein powder, and almond milk or soy milk in the Ninja Creami Deluxe blender pitcher until smooth.
2. Pour the smoothie into a bowl.
3. Top with sliced banana, a drizzle of peanut butter, chopped peanuts, and chocolate chips.
4. Serve immediately.

Nutritional Information:

- Calories: 400 kcal
- Protein: 30g
- Carbohydrates: 45g
- Fat: 15g
- Fiber: 8g

Raspberry Almond Protein Smoothie Bowl

- **Prep Time:** 5 minutes

- **Serving Size:** 1 bowl

Ingredients:

- 1 cup frozen raspberries

- 1/2 banana, frozen

- 1 scoop vanilla or almond-flavored protein powder

- 1/2 cup almond milk or Greek yogurt

- Toppings: fresh raspberries, sliced almonds, almond butter drizzle, shredded coconut

Instructions:

1. Blend the frozen raspberries, frozen banana, vanilla or almond-flavored protein powder, and almond milk or Greek yogurt in the Ninja Creami Deluxe blender pitcher until smooth.

2. Pour the smoothie into a bowl.

3. Top with fresh raspberries, sliced almonds, a drizzle of almond butter, and shredded coconut.

4. Serve immediately.

Nutritional Information:

- Calories: 350 kcal

- Protein: 28g

- Carbohydrates: 45g

- Fat: 10g

- Fiber: 10g

Chapter 8: Candy and Cookie Recipes

Protein Peanut Butter Cups

- **Prep Time:** 15 minutes
- **Cook Time:** 0 minutes (chilling time required)
- **Serving Size:** 12 pieces

Ingredients:

- 1 cup creamy peanut butter
- 1/4 cup honey or maple syrup
- 1 scoop vanilla or chocolate protein powder
- 1/2 cup dark chocolate chips
- Sea salt (optional)

Instructions:

1. In a bowl, mix together the peanut butter, honey or maple syrup, and protein powder until well combined.
2. Line a muffin tin with paper liners.
3. Melt the dark chocolate chips in a microwave-safe bowl in 30-second intervals, stirring in between until smooth.
4. Spoon a small amount of melted chocolate into each paper liner, spreading it to coat the bottom.
5. Place a spoonful of the peanut butter mixture on top of the chocolate layer in each liner.
6. Cover the peanut butter layer with the remaining melted chocolate.
7. Sprinkle a pinch of sea salt on top if desired.
8. Chill in the refrigerator for at least 2 hours or until firm.
9. Once set, remove the paper liners and serve.

Nutritional Information per Serving (1 piece):

- Calories: 150 kcal

- Protein: 6g

- Carbohydrates: 10g

- Fat: 10g

- Fiber: 2g

Protein Chocolate Chip Cookies

- **Prep Time:** 10 minutes

- **Cook Time:** 10-12 minutes

- **Serving Size:** 12 cookies

Ingredients:

- 1 cup almond flour

- 1 scoop vanilla or chocolate protein powder

- 1/4 cup coconut oil, melted

- 1/4 cup honey or maple syrup

- 1/2 teaspoon baking soda

- 1/4 teaspoon salt

- 1/3 cup dark chocolate chips

Instructions:

1. Preheat your oven to 350°F (175°C) and line a baking sheet with parchment paper.

2. In a bowl, combine the almond flour, protein powder, melted coconut oil, honey or maple syrup, baking soda, and salt. Mix until a dough forms.

3. Fold in the dark chocolate chips.

4. Scoop tablespoon-sized portions of dough onto the prepared baking sheet, spacing them apart.

5. Flatten each cookie slightly with the back of a spoon.

6. Bake for 10-12 minutes or until the edges are golden brown.

7. Remove from the oven and let cool on the baking sheet for 5 minutes before transferring to a wire rack to cool completely.

Nutritional Information per Serving (1 cookie):

- Calories: 140 kcal

- Protein: 5g

- Carbohydrates: 10g

- Fat: 9g

- Fiber: 1g

Protein Almond Joy Bites

- **Prep Time:** 20 minutes

- **Cook Time:** 0 minutes (chilling time required)

- **Serving Size:** 12 bites

Ingredients:

- 1 cup shredded coconut (unsweetened)

- 1/4 cup almond flour

- 1/4 cup honey or maple syrup

- 1 scoop vanilla or coconut-flavored protein powder

- 1/4 cup almond butter

- 1/2 cup dark chocolate chips

- 1 tablespoon coconut oil

Instructions:

1. In a bowl, mix together the shredded coconut, almond flour, honey or maple syrup, protein powder, and almond butter until well combined.

2. Roll the mixture into bite-sized balls and place them on a baking sheet lined with parchment paper.

3. Freeze the coconut balls for 10-15 minutes to firm up.

4. In the meantime, melt the dark chocolate chips and coconut oil together in a microwave-safe bowl in 30-second intervals, stirring until smooth.

5. Dip each frozen coconut ball into the melted chocolate to coat evenly, using a fork or spoon to remove excess chocolate.

6. Place the coated balls back on the parchment-lined baking sheet.

7. Chill in the refrigerator for at least 30 minutes or until the chocolate coating is set.

8. Serve chilled.

Nutritional Information per Serving (1 bite):

- Calories: 150 kcal

- Protein: 5g

- Carbohydrates: 10g

- Fat: 11g

- Fiber: 2g

Protein Oatmeal Raisin Cookies

- **Prep Time:** 15 minutes

- **Cook Time:** 12-15 minutes

- **Serving Size:** 12 cookies

Ingredients:

- 1 cup rolled oats

- 1/2 cup almond flour

- 1 scoop vanilla or cinnamon-flavored protein powder

- 1/4 cup coconut oil, melted

- 1/4 cup honey or maple syrup

- 1/2 teaspoon baking soda

- 1/2 teaspoon ground cinnamon

- 1/4 teaspoon salt

- 1/3 cup raisins

Instructions:

1. Preheat your oven to 350°F (175°C) and line a baking sheet with parchment paper.

2. In a bowl, mix together the rolled oats, almond flour, protein powder, melted coconut oil, honey or maple syrup, baking soda, cinnamon, and salt until combined.

3. Fold in the raisins.

4. Scoop tablespoon-sized portions of dough onto the prepared baking sheet, spacing them apart.

5. Flatten each cookie slightly with the back of a spoon.

6. Bake for 12-15 minutes or until golden brown.

7. Remove from the oven and let cool on the baking sheet for 5 minutes before transferring to a wire rack to cool completely.

Nutritional Information per Serving (1 cookie):

- Calories: 140 kcal

- Protein: 5g

- Carbohydrates: 15g

- Fat: 7g

- Fiber: 2g

Protein Mint Chocolate Truffles

- **Prep Time:** 20 minutes

- **Cook Time:** 0 minutes (chilling time required)

- **Serving Size:** 12 truffles

Ingredients:

- 1 cup almond flour

- 1/4 cup cocoa powder (unsweetened)

- 1 scoop chocolate or mint-flavored protein powder

- 1/4 cup honey or maple syrup

- 1/4 cup coconut oil, melted

- 1/2 teaspoon peppermint extract (optional)

- 1/3 cup dark chocolate chips

- Crushed candy canes (optional, for coating)

Instructions:

1. In a bowl, combine the almond flour, cocoa powder, protein powder, honey or maple syrup, melted coconut oil, and peppermint extract (if using) until a dough forms.

2. Roll the dough into tablespoon-sized balls and place them on a baking sheet lined with parchment paper.

3. Freeze the truffles for 10-15 minutes to firm up.

4. In the meantime, melt the dark chocolate chips in a microwave-safe bowl in 30-second intervals, stirring until smooth.

5. Dip each frozen truffle into the melted chocolate, coating them evenly. You can use a fork or spoon to remove excess chocolate.

6. Place the coated truffles back on the parchment-lined baking sheet.

7. Optional: Sprinkle crushed candy canes on top of the truffles before the chocolate sets for a festive touch.

8. Chill the truffles in the refrigerator for at least 30 minutes or until the chocolate coating is firm.

9. Serve chilled and enjoy!

Nutritional Information per Serving (1 truffle):

- Calories: 150 kcal

- Protein: 5g

- Carbohydrates: 15g

- Fat: 9g

- Fiber: 2g

Protein Snickerdoodle Energy Balls

- **Prep Time:** 15 minutes

- **Cook Time:** 0 minutes (chilling time required)

- **Serving Size:** 12 balls

Ingredients:

- 1 cup almond flour

- 1 scoop vanilla or cinnamon-flavored protein powder

- 1/4 cup honey or maple syrup

- 2 tablespoons coconut oil, melted

- 1 teaspoon ground cinnamon

- 1/2 teaspoon vanilla extract

- 2 tablespoons granulated sugar (for coating)

Instructions:

1. In a bowl, mix together the almond flour, protein powder, honey or maple syrup, melted coconut oil, ground cinnamon, and vanilla extract until well combined.

2. Roll the mixture into tablespoon-sized balls and place them on a plate.

3. In a separate small bowl, mix the granulated sugar and a little extra cinnamon (if desired) for coating.

4. Roll each energy ball in the cinnamon sugar mixture until coated evenly.

5. Place the coated balls on a parchment-lined baking sheet.

6. Chill the energy balls in the refrigerator for at least 30 minutes to firm up.

7. Serve chilled or at room temperature.

Nutritional Information per Serving (1 ball):

- Calories: 120 kcal

- Protein: 5g

- Carbohydrates: 10g

- Fat: 7g

- Fiber: 2g

Protein Coconut Macaroons

- **Prep Time:** 15 minutes

- **Cook Time:** 12-15 minutes

- **Serving Size:** 12 macaroons

Ingredients:

- 2 cups shredded coconut (unsweetened)

- 1/2 cup almond flour

- 1 scoop vanilla or coconut-flavored protein powder

- 1/2 cup honey or maple syrup

- 1/4 cup coconut oil, melted

- 1 teaspoon vanilla extract

- Pinch of salt

Instructions:

1. Preheat your oven to 350°F (175°C) and line a baking sheet with parchment paper.

2. In a bowl, combine the shredded coconut, almond flour, protein powder, honey or maple syrup, melted coconut oil, vanilla extract, and a pinch of salt until well mixed.

3. Scoop tablespoon-sized portions of the mixture and shape them into macaroon-like balls or use a cookie scoop to form them.

4. Place the macaroons on the prepared baking sheet, spacing them apart.

5. Bake for 12-15 minutes or until the edges are golden brown.

6. Remove from the oven and let cool on the baking sheet for 5 minutes before transferring to a wire rack to cool completely.

Nutritional Information per Serving (1 macaroon):

- Calories: 150 kcal

- Protein: 4g

- Carbohydrates: 12g

- Fat: 10g

- Fiber: 2g

Protein Chocolate Bark

- **Prep Time:** 10 minutes

- **Cook Time:** 0 minutes (chilling time required)

- **Serving Size:** Varies

Ingredients:

- 1 cup dark chocolate chips

- 1 scoop chocolate or vanilla protein powder

- 1/4 cup mixed nuts and dried fruits (e.g., almonds, walnuts, dried cranberries, raisins)

- Pinch of sea salt (optional)

Instructions:

1. Line a baking sheet with parchment paper.

2. Melt the dark chocolate chips in a microwave-safe bowl in 30-second intervals, stirring until smooth.

3. Once melted, stir in the protein powder until well combined.

4. Pour the chocolate mixture onto the prepared baking sheet and spread it out evenly with a spatula.

5. Sprinkle the mixed nuts, dried fruits, and a pinch of sea salt (if using) over the chocolate layer.

6. Chill the chocolate bark in the refrigerator for at least 1 hour or until firm.

7. Once set, break the bark into pieces of desired size.

Nutritional Information per Serving (varies based on serving size):

- Calories: Varies

- Protein: Varies

- Carbohydrates: Varies

- Fat: Varies

- Fiber: Varies

Protein Chocolate-Coconut Truffles

- **Prep Time:** 20 minutes

- **Cook Time:** 0 minutes (chilling time required)

- **Serving Size:** 12 truffles

Ingredients:

- 1 cup shredded coconut (unsweetened)

- 1/4 cup coconut oil, melted

- 1 scoop chocolate or coconut-flavored protein powder

- 1/4 cup honey or maple syrup

- 1/3 cup dark chocolate chips

- Crushed almonds or pistachios (for coating)

Instructions:

1. In a bowl, mix together the shredded coconut, melted coconut oil, protein powder, and honey or maple syrup until well combined.

2. Roll the mixture into tablespoon-sized balls and place them on a baking sheet lined with parchment paper.

3. Freeze the coconut balls for 10-15 minutes to firm up.

4. In the meantime, melt the dark chocolate chips in a microwave-safe bowl in 30-second intervals, stirring until smooth.

5. Dip each frozen coconut ball into the melted chocolate to coat evenly, using a fork or spoon to remove excess chocolate.

6. Roll the coated balls in crushed almonds or pistachios for added texture and flavor.

7. Place the coated truffles back on the parchment-lined baking sheet.

8. Chill in the refrigerator for at least 30 minutes or until the chocolate coating is set.

9. Serve chilled and enjoy!

Nutritional Information per Serving (1 truffle):

- Calories: 150 kcal

- Protein: 5g

- Carbohydrates: 10g

- Fat: 11g

- Fiber: 2g

Protein-Packed Rice Krispie Treats

- **Prep Time:** 15 minutes

- **Cook Time:** 5 minutes

- **Serving Size:** 12 bars

Ingredients:

- 4 cups crispy rice cereal

- 1/2 cup honey or maple syrup

- 1/2 cup almond butter or peanut butter

- 1 scoop vanilla or chocolate protein powder

- 1/4 cup dark chocolate chips (optional)

- Cooking spray (for greasing)

Instructions:

1. Grease a 9x9-inch baking pan with cooking spray and set aside.

2. In a large mixing bowl, combine the crispy rice cereal and protein powder. Set aside.

3. In a saucepan over low heat, warm the honey or maple syrup and almond butter or peanut butter until well combined and smooth, stirring constantly.

4. Pour the warm honey/almond butter mixture over the crispy rice cereal and protein powder mixture. Stir until everything is evenly coated.

5. If using, fold in the dark chocolate chips into the mixture.

6. Transfer the mixture to the greased baking pan and press it down evenly using a spatula or your hands.

7. Chill in the refrigerator for at least 1 hour or until firm.

8. Once set, cut into bars or squares and serve.

Nutritional Information per Serving (1 bar):

- Calories: 200 kcal

- Protein: 8g

- Carbohydrates: 25g

- Fat: 8g

- Fiber: 2g

Chapter 9: Creamy Creamiccinos Recipes

Vanilla Protein Creamiccino

- **Prep Time:** 5 minutes

- **Cook Time:** 0 minutes

- **Serving Size:** 1 serving

Ingredients:

- 1 cup brewed coffee, chilled

- 1/2 cup almond milk

- 1 scoop vanilla protein powder

- 1 tablespoon unsweetened cocoa powder (optional)

- Ice cubes

- Whipped cream (optional topping)

- Cinnamon powder (optional topping)

Instructions:

1. In the Ninja Creami Deluxe blender pitcher, combine the chilled brewed coffee, almond milk, vanilla protein powder, and unsweetened cocoa powder (if using).

2. Add ice cubes to reach your desired thickness and blend until smooth and creamy.

3. Pour the Creamiccino into a glass.

4. Optional: Top with whipped cream and a sprinkle of cinnamon powder.

5. Serve immediately and enjoy!

Nutritional Information per Serving:

- Calories: 120 kcal

- Protein: 15g

- Carbohydrates: 5g

- Fat: 4g

- Fiber: 2g

Chocolate Protein Creamiccino

- **Prep Time:** 5 minutes

- **Cook Time:** 0 minutes

- **Serving Size:** 1 serving

Ingredients:

- 1 cup brewed coffee, chilled

- 1/2 cup milk of choice (e.g., almond milk, soy milk)

- 1 scoop chocolate protein powder

- 1 tablespoon sugar-free chocolate syrup

- Ice cubes

- Whipped cream (optional topping)

- Cocoa powder (optional topping)

Instructions:

1. In the Ninja Creami Deluxe blender pitcher, combine the chilled brewed coffee, milk of choice, chocolate protein powder, and sugar-free chocolate syrup.

2. Add ice cubes to reach your desired consistency and blend until smooth and creamy.

3. Pour the Chocolate Creamiccino into a glass.

4. Optional: Top with whipped cream and a sprinkle of cocoa powder.

5. Serve immediately and enjoy!

Nutritional Information per Serving:

- Calories: 150 kcal

- Protein: 18g

- Carbohydrates: 8g

- Fat: 5g

- Fiber: 3g

Caramel Protein Creamiccino

- **Prep Time:** 5 minutes

- **Cook Time:** 0 minutes

- **Serving Size:** 1 serving

Ingredients:

- 1 cup brewed coffee, chilled

- 1/2 cup milk of choice (e.g., coconut milk, cashew milk)

- 1 scoop caramel-flavored protein powder

- 1 tablespoon sugar-free caramel syrup

- Ice cubes

- Whipped cream (optional topping)

- Caramel drizzle (optional topping)

Instructions:

1. In the Ninja Creami Deluxe blender pitcher, combine the chilled brewed coffee, milk of choice, caramel-flavored protein powder, and sugar-free caramel syrup.

2. Add ice cubes to reach your desired thickness and blend until creamy and well combined.

3. Pour the Caramel Creamiccino into a glass.

4. Optional: Top with whipped cream and a drizzle of caramel syrup.

5. Serve immediately and enjoy!

Nutritional Information per Serving:

- Calories: 140 kcal

- Protein: 17g

- Carbohydrates: 6g

- Fat: 5g

- Fiber: 1g

Mocha Protein Creamiccino

- **Prep Time:** 5 minutes

- **Cook Time:** 0 minutes

- **Serving Size:** 1 serving

Ingredients:

- 1 cup brewed coffee, chilled

- 1/2 cup milk of choice (e.g., almond milk, oat milk)

- 1 scoop chocolate protein powder

- 1 tablespoon sugar-free mocha syrup

- Ice cubes

- Whipped cream (optional topping)

- Chocolate shavings (optional topping)

Instructions:

1. In the Ninja Creami Deluxe blender pitcher, combine the chilled brewed coffee, milk of choice, chocolate protein powder, and sugar-free mocha syrup.

2. Add ice cubes to reach your desired consistency and blend until smooth and frothy.

3. Pour the Mocha Creamiccino into a glass.

4. Optional: Top with whipped cream and a sprinkle of chocolate shavings.

5. Serve immediately and enjoy!

Nutritional Information per Serving:

- Calories: 130 kcal

- Protein: 16g

- Carbohydrates: 7g

- Fat: 4g

- Fiber: 2g

Hazelnut Protein Creamiccino

- **Prep Time:** 5 minutes

- **Cook Time:** 0 minutes

- **Serving Size:** 1 serving

Ingredients:

- 1 cup brewed coffee, chilled

- 1/2 cup milk of choice (e.g., soy milk, coconut milk)

- 1 scoop hazelnut-flavored protein powder

- 1 tablespoon sugar-free hazelnut syrup

- Ice cubes

- Whipped cream (optional topping)

- Ground cinnamon (optional topping)

Instructions:

1. In the Ninja Creami Deluxe blender pitcher, combine the chilled brewed coffee, milk of choice, hazelnut-flavored protein powder, and sugar-free hazelnut syrup.

2. Add ice cubes to achieve the desired thickness and blend until smooth and creamy.

3. Pour the Hazelnut Creamiccino into a glass.

4. Optional: Top with whipped cream and a sprinkle of ground cinnamon.

5. Serve immediately and enjoy!

Nutritional Information per Serving:

- Calories: 150 kcal

- Protein: 18g

- Carbohydrates: 7g

- Fat: 5g

- Fiber: 2g

Raspberry Vanilla Protein Creamiccino

- **Prep Time:** 5 minutes

- **Cook Time:** 0 minutes

- **Serving Size:** 1 serving

Ingredients:

- 1 cup brewed coffee, chilled

- 1/2 cup milk of choice (e.g., almond milk, cashew milk)

- 1 scoop vanilla protein powder

- 1/4 cup fresh or frozen raspberries

- Ice cubes

- Whipped cream (optional topping)

- Fresh raspberries (optional topping)

Instructions:

1. In the Ninja Creami Deluxe blender pitcher, combine the chilled brewed coffee, milk of choice, vanilla protein powder, and fresh or frozen raspberries.

2. Add ice cubes to reach your desired consistency and blend until smooth and creamy.

3. Pour the Raspberry Vanilla Creamiccino into a glass.

4. Optional: Top with whipped cream and fresh raspberries.

5. Serve immediately and enjoy!

Nutritional Information per Serving:

- Calories: 140 kcal

- Protein: 16g

- Carbohydrates: 8g

- Fat: 4g

- Fiber: 2g

Blueberry Protein Creamiccino

- **Prep Time:** 5 minutes

- **Cook Time:** 0 minutes

- **Serving Size:** 1 serving

Ingredients:

- 1 cup brewed coffee, chilled

- 1/2 cup milk of choice (e.g., soy milk, almond milk)

- 1 scoop vanilla or blueberry-flavored protein powder

- 1/4 cup fresh or frozen blueberries

- Ice cubes

- Whipped cream (optional topping)

- Fresh blueberries (optional topping)

Instructions:

1. In the Ninja Creami Deluxe blender pitcher, combine the chilled brewed coffee, milk of choice, vanilla or blueberry-flavored protein powder, and fresh or frozen blueberries.

2. Add ice cubes to reach your desired consistency and blend until smooth and creamy.

3. Pour the Blueberry Creamiccino into a glass.

4. Optional: Top with whipped cream and fresh blueberries.

5. Serve immediately and enjoy!

Nutritional Information per Serving:

- Calories: 130 kcal

- Protein: 15g

- Carbohydrates: 8g

- Fat: 4g

- Fiber: 2g

Peanut Butter Protein Creamiccino

- **Prep Time:** 5 minutes

- **Cook Time:** 0 minutes

- **Serving Size:** 1 serving

Ingredients:

- 1 cup brewed coffee, chilled

- 1/2 cup milk of choice (e.g., cashew milk, coconut milk)

- 1 scoop vanilla or chocolate protein powder

- 1 tablespoon natural peanut butter

- Ice cubes

- Whipped cream (optional topping)

- Crushed peanuts (optional topping)

Instructions:

1. In the Ninja Creami Deluxe blender pitcher, combine the chilled brewed coffee, milk of choice, vanilla or chocolate protein powder, and natural peanut butter.

2. Add ice cubes to achieve the desired thickness and blend until smooth and creamy.

3. Pour the Peanut Butter Creamiccino into a glass.

4. Optional: Top with whipped cream and crushed peanuts.

5. Serve immediately and enjoy!

Nutritional Information per Serving:

- Calories: 160 kcal

- Protein: 18g

- Carbohydrates: 7g

- Fat: 7g

- Fiber: 2g

Banana Protein Creamiccino

- **Prep Time:** 5 minutes

- **Cook Time:** 0 minutes

- **Serving Size:** 1 serving

Ingredients:

- 1 cup brewed coffee, chilled

- 1/2 cup milk of choice (e.g., almond milk, soy milk)

- 1 scoop vanilla or banana-flavored protein powder

- 1/2 ripe banana

- Ice cubes

- Whipped cream (optional topping)

- Banana slices (optional topping)

Instructions:

1. In the Ninja Creami Deluxe blender pitcher, combine the chilled brewed coffee, milk of choice, vanilla or banana-flavored protein powder, and ripe banana.

2. Add ice cubes to achieve the desired consistency and blend until smooth and creamy.

3. Pour the Banana Creamiccino into a glass.

4. Optional: Top with whipped cream and banana slices.

5. Serve immediately and enjoy!

Nutritional Information per Serving:

- Calories: 140 kcal

- Protein: 16g

- Carbohydrates: 9g

- Fat: 4g

- Fiber: 2g

Coconut Protein Creamiccino

- **Prep Time:** 5 minutes

- **Cook Time:** 0 minutes

- **Serving Size:** 1 serving

Ingredients:

- 1 cup brewed coffee, chilled

- 1/2 cup coconut milk

- 1 scoop vanilla or coconut-flavored protein powder

- 1 tablespoon unsweetened coconut flakes

- Ice cubes

- Whipped cream (optional topping)

- Toasted coconut flakes (optional topping)

Instructions:

1. In the Ninja Creami Deluxe blender pitcher, combine the chilled brewed coffee, coconut milk, vanilla or coconut-flavored protein powder, and unsweetened coconut flakes.

2. Add ice cubes to achieve the desired thickness and blend until smooth and creamy.

3. Pour the Coconut Creamiccino into a glass.

4. Optional: Top with whipped cream and toasted coconut flakes.

5. Serve immediately and enjoy!

Nutritional Information per Serving:

- Calories: 140 kcal
- Protein: 15g
- Carbohydrates: 6g
- Fat: 7g

- Fiber: 2g

Chapter 10: Italian Ice Cream

Lemon Basil Italian Ice

- **Prep Time:** 10 minutes
- **Freeze Time:** 4-6 hours
- **Serving Size:** 4 servings

Ingredients:

- 2 cups water
- 1 cup fresh lemon juice
- Zest of 1 lemon
- 1/2 cup granulated sugar (adjust to taste)
- 1/4 cup fresh basil leaves, chopped
- 1 scoop lemon-flavored protein powder (optional for added protein)

Instructions:

1. In a saucepan, combine water, lemon juice, lemon zest, and sugar. Heat over medium heat until the sugar dissolves completely, stirring occasionally.

2. Remove from heat and stir in the chopped basil leaves. Let the mixture cool to room temperature.

3. Pour the mixture into ice cube trays or a shallow freezer-safe dish. Freeze for about 2 hours or until partially frozen.

4. Transfer the partially frozen mixture to the Ninja Creami Deluxe blender pitcher. Add the lemon-flavored protein powder if using.

5. Blend until smooth and creamy.

6. Pour the Lemon Basil Italian Ice into serving bowls or cups.

7. Garnish with fresh basil leaves or lemon zest if desired.

8. Serve immediately and enjoy!

Nutritional Information per Serving:

- Calories: 80 kcal

- Protein: 5g

- Carbohydrates: 20g

- Fat: 0g

- Fiber: 1g

Strawberry Balsamic Italian Ice

- **Prep Time:** 15 minutes

- **Freeze Time:** 4-6 hours

- **Serving Size:** 4 servings

Ingredients:

- 2 cups fresh strawberries, hulled and halved

- 1/4 cup balsamic vinegar

- 1/4 cup honey or agave syrup

- 1 scoop vanilla or strawberry-flavored protein powder (optional)

- Fresh mint leaves for garnish

Instructions:

1. In a blender, combine fresh strawberries, balsamic vinegar, and honey or agave syrup. Blend until smooth.

2. Pour the mixture into ice cube trays or a shallow freezer-safe dish. Freeze for about 2 hours or until partially frozen.

3. Transfer the partially frozen mixture to the Ninja Creami Deluxe blender pitcher. Add the vanilla or strawberry-flavored protein powder if using.

4. Blend until smooth and creamy.

5. Pour the Strawberry Balsamic Italian Ice into serving bowls or cups.

6. Garnish with fresh mint leaves.

7. Serve immediately and enjoy!

Nutritional Information per Serving:

- Calories: 90 kcal

- Protein: 3g

- Carbohydrates: 22g

- Fat: 0g

- Fiber: 2g

Mango Coconut Italian Ice

- **Prep Time:** 10 minutes

- **Freeze Time:** 4-6 hours

- **Serving Size:** 4 servings

Ingredients:

- 2 cups frozen mango chunks

- 1/2 cup coconut milk

- 1/4 cup honey or maple syrup

- 1 scoop coconut-flavored protein powder (optional)

- Toasted coconut flakes for garnish

Instructions:

1. In a blender, combine frozen mango chunks, coconut milk, and honey or maple syrup. Blend until smooth.

2. Pour the mixture into ice cube trays or a shallow freezer-safe dish. Freeze for about 2 hours or until partially frozen.

3. Transfer the partially frozen mixture to the Ninja Creami Deluxe blender pitcher. Add the coconut-flavored protein powder if using.

4. Blend until smooth and creamy.

5. Pour the Mango Coconut Italian Ice into serving bowls or cups.

6. Garnish with toasted coconut flakes.

7. Serve immediately and enjoy!

Nutritional Information per Serving:

- Calories: 120 kcal

- Protein: 4g

- Carbohydrates: 25g

- Fat: 2g

- Fiber: 3g

Raspberry Lime Italian Ice

- **Prep Time:** 15 minutes

- **Freeze Time:** 4-6 hours

- **Serving Size:** 4 servings

Ingredients:

- 2 cups fresh or frozen raspberries

- Juice of 2 limes

- Zest of 1 lime

- 1/4 cup honey or agave syrup

- 1 scoop lime-flavored protein powder (optional)

- Fresh raspberries for garnish

Instructions:

1. In a blender, combine fresh or frozen raspberries, lime juice, lime zest, and honey or agave syrup. Blend until smooth.

2. Pour the mixture into ice cube trays or a shallow freezer-safe dish. Freeze for about 2 hours or until partially frozen.

3. Transfer the partially frozen mixture to the Ninja Creami Deluxe blender pitcher. Add the lime-flavored protein powder if using.

4. Blend until smooth and creamy.

5. Pour the Raspberry Lime Italian Ice into serving bowls or cups.

6. Garnish with fresh raspberries.

7. Serve immediately and enjoy!

Nutritional Information per Serving:

- Calories: 80 kcal

- Protein: 3g

- Carbohydrates: 20g

- Fat: 0g

- Fiber: 4g

Watermelon Mint Italian Ice

- **Prep Time:** 10 minutes

- **Freeze Time:** 4-6 hours

- **Serving Size:** 4 servings

Ingredients:

- 4 cups seedless watermelon, cubed

- Juice of 1 lime

- Zest of 1 lime

- 1/4 cup honey or agave syrup

- Fresh mint leaves for garnish

Instructions:

1. In a blender, combine watermelon cubes, lime juice, lime zest, and honey or agave syrup. Blend until smooth.

2. Pour the mixture into ice cube trays or a shallow freezer-safe dish. Freeze for about 2 hours or until partially frozen.

3. Transfer the partially frozen mixture to the Ninja Creami Deluxe blender pitcher.

4. Blend until smooth and creamy.

5. Pour the Watermelon Mint Italian Ice into serving bowls or cups.

6. Garnish with fresh mint leaves.

7. Serve immediately and enjoy!

Nutritional Information per Serving:

- Calories: 70 kcal

- Protein: 1g

- Carbohydrates: 18g

- Fat: 0g

- Fiber: 1g

Pineapple Coconut Italian Ice

- **Prep Time:** 10 minutes

- **Freeze Time:** 4-6 hours

- **Serving Size:** 4 servings

Ingredients:

- 2 cups frozen pineapple chunks

- 1/2 cup coconut water

- 1/4 cup coconut cream

- 1 scoop coconut-flavored protein powder (optional)

- Toasted coconut flakes for garnish

Instructions:

1. In a blender, combine frozen pineapple chunks, coconut water, and coconut cream. Blend until smooth.

2. Pour the mixture into ice cube trays or a shallow freezer-safe dish. Freeze for about 2 hours or until partially frozen.

3. Transfer the partially frozen mixture to the Ninja Creami Deluxe blender pitcher. Add the coconut-flavored protein powder if using.

4. Blend until smooth and creamy.

5. Pour the Pineapple Coconut Italian Ice into serving bowls or cups.

6. Garnish with toasted coconut flakes.

7. Serve immediately and enjoy!

Nutritional Information per Serving:

- Calories: 100 kcal

- Protein: 2g

- Carbohydrates: 20g

- Fat: 2g

- Fiber: 2g

Blueberry Lemon Italian Ice

- **Prep Time:** 15 minutes

- **Freeze Time:** 4-6 hours

- **Serving Size:** 4 servings

Ingredients:

- 2 cups fresh or frozen blueberries

- Juice of 2 lemons

- Zest of 1 lemon

- 1/4 cup honey or agave syrup

- 1 scoop lemon-flavored protein powder (optional)

- Fresh blueberries for garnish

Instructions:

1. In a blender, combine fresh or frozen blueberries, lemon juice, lemon zest, and honey or agave syrup. Blend until smooth.

2. Pour the mixture into ice cube trays or a shallow freezer-safe dish. Freeze for about 2 hours or until partially frozen.

3. Transfer the partially frozen mixture to the Ninja Creami Deluxe blender pitcher. Add the lemon-flavored protein powder if using.

4. Blend until smooth and creamy.

5. Pour the Blueberry Lemon Italian Ice into serving bowls or cups.

6. Garnish with fresh blueberries.

7. Serve immediately and enjoy!

Nutritional Information per Serving:

- Calories: 90 kcal

- Protein: 3g

- Carbohydrates: 22g

- Fat: 0g

- Fiber: 3g

Peach Mango Italian Ice

- **Prep Time:** 10 minutes

- **Freeze Time:** 4-6 hours

- **Serving Size:** 4 servings

Ingredients:

- 2 cups frozen mango chunks

- 1 cup frozen peach slices

- 1/4 cup honey or agave syrup

- 1 scoop vanilla or mango-flavored protein powder (optional)

- Fresh mint leaves for garnish

Instructions:

1. In a blender, combine frozen mango chunks, frozen peach slices, and honey or agave syrup. Blend until smooth.

2. Pour the mixture into ice cube trays or a shallow freezer-safe dish. Freeze for about 2 hours or until partially frozen.

3. Transfer the partially frozen mixture to the Ninja Creami Deluxe blender pitcher. Add the vanilla or mango-flavored protein powder if using.

4. Blend until smooth and creamy.

5. Pour the Peach Mango Italian Ice into serving bowls or cups.

6. Garnish with fresh mint leaves.

7. Serve immediately and enjoy!

Nutritional Information per Serving:

- Calories: 110 kcal
- Protein: 2g
- Carbohydrates: 28g
- Fat: 0g

- Fiber: 3g

Kiwi Lime Italian Ice

- **Prep Time:** 15 minutes

- **Freeze Time:** 4-6 hours

- **Serving Size:** 4 servings

Ingredients:

- 4 ripe kiwis, peeled and diced

- Juice of 2 limes

- Zest of 1 lime

- 1/4 cup honey or agave syrup

- 1 scoop lime-flavored protein powder (optional)

- Kiwi slices for garnish

Instructions:

1. In a blender, combine diced kiwis, lime juice, lime zest, and honey or agave syrup. Blend until smooth.

2. Pour the mixture into ice cube trays or a shallow freezer-safe dish. Freeze for about 2 hours or until partially frozen.

3. Transfer the partially frozen mixture to the Ninja Creami Deluxe blender pitcher. Add the lime-flavored protein powder if using.

4. Blend until smooth and creamy.

5. Pour the Kiwi Lime Italian Ice into serving bowls or cups.

6. Garnish with kiwi slices.

7. Serve immediately and enjoy!

Nutritional Information per Serving:

- Calories: 100 kcal

- Protein: 3g

- Carbohydrates: 25g

- Fat: 0g

- Fiber: 3g

Mixed Berry Italian Ice

- **Prep Time:** 15 minutes

- **Freeze Time:** 4-6 hours

- **Serving Size:** 4 servings

Ingredients:

- 2 cups mixed berries (such as strawberries, blueberries, raspberries)

- 1/4 cup honey or agave syrup

- Juice of 1 lemon

- Zest of 1 lemon

- 1 scoop mixed berry-flavored protein powder (optional)

- Fresh berries for garnish

Instructions:

1. In a blender, combine mixed berries, honey or agave syrup, lemon juice, and lemon zest. Blend until smooth.

2. Pour the mixture into ice cube trays or a shallow freezer-safe dish. Freeze for about 2 hours or until partially frozen.

3. Transfer the partially frozen mixture to the Ninja Creami Deluxe blender pitcher. Add the mixed berry-flavored protein powder if using.

4. Blend until smooth and creamy.

5. Pour the Mixed Berry Italian Ice into serving bowls or cups.

6. Garnish with fresh berries.

7. Serve immediately and enjoy!

Nutritional Information per Serving:

- Calories: 90 kcal

- Protein: 2g

- Carbohydrates: 23g

- Fat: 0g

- Fiber: 4g

Conclusion

The Ninja Creami Deluxe High Protein Recipes Cookbook includes a delightful selection of frozen pleasures that are not only delicious but also high in protein, making them ideal for anybody trying to maintain a balanced and nutritious diet. From velvety Creamiccinos to cool Italian Ice Adventure flavors, these recipes demonstrate the Ninja Creami Deluxe's versatility in making healthy yet delectable sweets.

These meals fulfill your appetites while also providing important nutrients to support your active lifestyle. Whether you're looking to refuel after a workout or indulge in a guilt-free dessert, the Ninja Creami Deluxe High Protein Recipes Cookbook has something for everyone.

This cookbook provides step-by-step instructions, nutritional information, and serving suggestions, making it simple to prepare these wonderful delicacies in the comfort of your own home. Say goodbye to store-bought frozen desserts and hello to handmade goodness with the Ninja Creami Deluxe!

We hope you enjoy trying out these recipes and creating delicious delicacies that nourish your health and satisfy your taste buds.

Made in United States
North Haven, CT
28 December 2024

63647314R00083